Islamism and Post-Islamism

Reflections upon
Allama Jafari's Political Thought

Seyed Javad Miri

University Press of America,® Inc.
Lanham • Boulder • New York • Toronto • Plymouth, UK

Copyright © 2014 by University Press of America,® Inc.
4501 Forbes Boulevard, Suite 200, Lanham, Maryland 20706
UPA Aquisitions Department (301) 459-3366

10 Thornbury Road, Plymouth PL6 7PP, United Kingdom

Library of Congress Control Number: 2014937725
ISBN: 978-0-7618-6387-8 (cloth : alk. paper)—ISBN: 978-0-7618-6388-5 (electronic)

Contents

Eurocentrism and Politics in a Critical Balance

Absence of Politics in the Empire of Islam

Designing of Social Life

5 Revisiting the Principle of Divine Authority

Politics and the Sunnite Interpretation

Revisiting the Principle of Divine Authority

Foreword

Our contemporary discourse concerning the topic of Islamism has been shaped primarily by western conceptions of Islamic fundamentalism, terrorism, and fanaticism. Islam itself, as a global religious tradition that guides and directs the lives of millions throughout the world, has been suspiciously leveled to a simplistic, monolithic, and culturally backward relic of the Middle East—an area of the world that has become increasingly incomprehensible to the western secular and non-religious worldview. For many, the demands of Islam exclusively take the form of jurisprudential pronouncements and violent outbursts at some perceived wrong; Muslims seems to be enraged over basic western values that allow westerners to freely criticize the sacred without regard to the offense that is given. Whereas the secular West, a product of the Enlightenment, de-sacralization, individualism, and modern capitalism, continuous views the Muslims world either with orientalist wonder or condemnatory dismissiveness, the Muslim world often stares back with prophetic angst against what they perceive as a complete disregard and disrespect of their religious views, cultural identity, and their right to determine their own being-in-the-world. As political tensions between East and West have increased, so too have the cultural misunderstandings. Islam, which for millions is a deeply rooted anchor in a world that seems to have lost its meta-physical moorings, is to others a dangerous ideology that confronts the modern world with the threat of a violent medieval mind-frame that harkens back before the beast of religion was domesticated in Europe. The beauty and majesty of Islam, the undiscovered and forgotten manifestation of the prophetic tradition of *tawhid* (التوحيد / divine oneness), remains behind a cultural veil in the blind eyes of secularity; whereas the abandonment of metaphysically legitimated morality, values, and principles, that make unconditional meaning possible, remains unfathomable to those who, in face of science, positivism, rationalism, and capitalism, continue to adhere to their faith. Despite the uneasiness of a faith within an increasingly faith-less world, the fundamental right of self-determination does not evaporate due to the pulsating antagonism between the sacred and the profane, or the Islamic and the non-Islamic. Muslims retain their rights to be who and what they are, no matter the state of the discourse with the rest of the world, but what truly matters within this discourse is not what the rest of the world thinks Muslims should be, but what do Muslims themselves want to be. If philoso-phers such as Jürgen Habermas implore us to engage in a robust exercise in mutual-perspective taking, then it is equally compelling that the Muslim community (*ummah*) must also engage in an intel-lectual civil war (*civile bellum intellectiva*)—but one that does not devour its young or humiliate the opposition—for both annihilation and humiliation make future reconciliation impossible. There must be an engaged discussion of the forms of politics that Islamism will take as it carves out a space for itself within the global public sphere—will it, as Seyed Javad Miri will ask, ghettoize itself within a jurisprudentialist approach, and willfully deprive the world of the spirit of Islamic compassion, mercy, and dignity? Would this not inevitably lead to an ossification and stagnation of Islam within its formal legal system? Or will it embrace a *demokratischen geist*; a more fluid, dynamic, and compassionate expression of the prophetic way-of-being-in-the-world. If the *ummah* chooses the first, Islam risks becoming a mere formal system of constrictions—a lifeless skeleton of lifeless laws—the "whitened sepulchers" that Jesus of Nazareth spoke of (Matthew 23:27). As the "priestly" overcomes the "prophetic," Islamic compassion (الرحمة الإسلامية) evaporates as the state becomes nearly devoid of all sympathy for the plight and predicament of its own community—its heart will harden. If it chooses the later, an Islamism infused with a democratic spirit, one that lends a sympathetic ear to the wishes and desires of the members of the *ummah*, then Islamism may be able to redeem itself from the negative images that plague its public life at the moment. When the Islamic state makes itself accountable to the δῆμος (demos—"people"), and derives its legitimacy from the will of the governed, as opposed to the *subjectively perceived* will of the divine, when it abandons the idea that it has the objective ability to rule in place of the messianic, then Islamism can be understood as a political-religious mode of being that is both Islamic and democratic. When critique of the state is separated from critique of Islam, only then can the Muslim world present a democratic Islamism as a legitimate form of socially organized governance that takes in account the issues of the modern world without romantically yearning for a past "Islamic garden of Eden" that never truly existed. The Muslim world must affix its eyes on a future-oriented remembrance of the past, with the practical intent to reduce the suffering of the *ummah* and increase the conditions for *eudaimonia* (εὐδαιμονία), *felicity* (felicitas), and *'adl* (عدل/justice). This prophetic vision that is rooted in the *sirah* (biography) of the Prophet Muhammad cannot be reimagined within the confines of an authoritarian and dictatorial ideologization of Islam. *Ideology*, if the tools of Critical Theory are consulted, is the purposeful masking of social and political antagonisms in an attempt to conceal the true nature of inequality, injustice, and oppression—exposing them to be the products of human thought and activity and not that of nature. When "Islamic" states abuse their governing powers, neglect their social responsibilities, and accumulate wealth and power at the expense of equality, justice, and the common good, doing so all in the name of Islam, the liberational and emancipatory potentials of Islam become muted if not stillborn. The public "face" of Islam and Islamism becomes infused with greed, distrust, oppression, and tyranny. One can hardly blame those in other parts of the non-Islamic world for their distorted view of Islam and Muslims; what other picture has been presented to them?

In terms of history, Islamism, as a political philosophy, can be distinguished from Islam as a religious tradition by the attitude in which it approaches the political realm of life. Islam, which has always had a political component to it since the time of the Prophet, has approached politics as another fully integrated sphere of social life that is deeply rooted in an existentially meaningful state of being. Politics was but one of many ways in which the Muslim community related to each other, entered into a vigorous discourses, and deliberated on the way in which a just and Islamic society should be ordered. The early Muslim community, including during the time of Prophet Muhammad, understood politics to be no more separate from the Islamic tradition than theology was from praxis. The compartmentalization of the lifeworld had not occurred and would not occur until the modern period. Ultimately, the political life was another expression of the embodiment of the Islamic ideal in the public sphere—it laid down the parameters in which the prophetic way of being in the world made possible the idea that Islam, as a social phenomenon, could establish a society that was embedded in justice, peace, and equality.

Nevertheless, even though the *sunnah* (way) and *sirah* (biography) of the prophet maintain a political component, Islamism, as a modern approach to the reaffirmation of Islamic politics, can be categorized as having a distinct quality that is lacking in the early Muslim community: it is in many ways a reaction to the dominating influence of western modernity. The history of the Muslim world under colonial and imperial occupation, through the *decolonization* period that left a political-economic structure in place that overwhelmingly benefited western powers (both government and corporate) while at the same time eliminating the physical presence of western occupation forces in the region, to the current unequivocal support of dictators and despots in the Middle East, has led many Muslim intellectuals, activists, and political actors to reassert the political component of the Islamic tradition back into global politics. Against the forced secularization of Turkey that attempted to erase the Islamic heritage of the Ottomans in favor of western culture and values, against the U.S. installed Shah of Iran as an agent of westernization and western political interests, against the continual "disenchantment of the world" that accompanies aggressive western capitalism and its rationalization and colonization of the lifeworld, Muslims have once again reasserted not only their identity as a community of believers, but also their desire to manifest a political reality that is rooted in their Islamic worldview. Muslims, beginning especially with the 1979 Islamic Revolution in Iran under the guidance of Ayatollah Khomeini, have demanded a certain *religious visibility,* as Seyed Javad Miri has demonstrated, in their societies. The invisibility of religion and religious sentiments in the western world, especially in those countries that find it part of their *modus operandi* to guard the citizenry from being exposed to religiosity, cannot be forced upon a civilization that does not separate the theological from the everyday—the indwelling of the divine in the world simply cannot be cancelled because it cannot be verified by another's dominant epistemology.

Nevertheless, Miri points out the dangers of *theologizing politics,* or inducing the sacredness and absoluteness of the divine into temporal and human activity, for it creates the potential for sanctified tyranny. To elevate what is mere-human polity to the certainty that the "divine wants it thusly" stifles the possibility for democratic deliberation on political matters—as it bars the citizenry from participating in the decision making that directly affects their lives. Political and social decisions made in such a way lack the democratic legitimacy that could render such policies acceptable by the governed, i.e. society itself. Furthermore, to fuse polity and theology without a democratic component with the power of oversight, can be a danger to both Islam and governance. When merged, to criticize the theologically legitimated political agent is to criticize the divine itself—as if the divine right of kings, long eliminated in the West via the Enlightenment's castration of theological legitimation, returns with a vengeance in the Muslim world. In the end, even if Islamism is the future, it must be infused, as Miri points out, with the spirit of deliberative democracy, which philosophically separates the source of legitimation from the particular actions of any given political actor. When the political takes on the heir of being divinely sanctioned, both the Islamic tradition and democracy are in peril, as the authoritarian potential within the theocratic polity renders all deliberation and critique as *heresy* and inherently *treasonous*, even if such critique is rooted in the prophetic-mode-of-being, which inherently questions the status quo of all power and structures of domination.

Furthermore, it may be the case that as Islamism moves towards a spirit of democracy and away from the *intellectual absurd* and *ecumenically resistant*, that it has too often embraced in totalitarian and authoritarian orientations, that it may need to discover "new translators"—those philosophers, sociologists, and activists who can skillfully render semantic and semiotic material from the depth of the Islamic tradition into a language that can be understood in the global context. In secular democracy, all arguments must be made with the use of "publically accessible reasoning" if it is going to be understood as a legitimate argument. In other words, there can be no appeal to religious metaphysics for justification or legitimacy—all attempts to win the other over to the better argument can only be done via the use of language that reason alone has access to—revelation cannot be the source of one's arguments as the legitimating *inner logic* of the sacred text is not accessible to those who are not already converted to that faith. For modern democratic Islamism, this can be a challenge when it wants to enter into the global public sphere. No appeal to the Qur'an can win over the secular democratic nations, just as an argument for the "inalienable" right of freedom of speech falls on the deaf ears of those with religious sensitivities; the right of religion and religious figures to be respected trumps the right of the "free" to disrespect them. Therefore, the language of Islam may have to shed its religious garb and enter into the global discourse on its own *rational* merits. Only reasonable arguments that do not rely on a system of religious metaphysics can win over the respect and admiration of the world—all peoples can speak and thinking rationally, but only Muslims can believe the in the absolute authority of the Qur'an and Islam. This fact bars many from considering the possibility that Muslims have something to offer the world other than the religiously inspired violence that is so often associated with Islamism. Thus the challenge of modern Islamism is twofold, 1) it must be infused with the democratic spirit, and 2) it must be able to communicate its concerns, values, principles, and beliefs in such a way that it is intelligible to the rest of the non-Muslim world. When Islamism has done these things, it has rendered a great service both to Islam and to the world.

Dustin Byrd
Professor of Humanities
Olivet College
USA
November, 2013

Preface

In May 2012, I was invited for an international conference in Moscow by the Russian Academy of Science where the participants wanted to inquire about eastern and western philosophical traditions. There I met a scholar from Turkey who presented a paper on Fetullah Gulen as the only authentic philosopher in the Muslim World. When his presentation was over I approached him and asked him if he knows about contemporary Iranian philosophers and social theorists. He got upset and told me that I should not have a fetishistic attachment to the past and I should wake up to the sour reality of today. He continued by preaching to me that "we do not have any real philosophers or social theorists today. The only thinker who is able to generate a sense of authenticity among us is Fetullah Gulen." I tried to dialog with him by mentioning few names of contemporary Iranian thinkers, intellectuals and philosophers but he refused to listen. His answer was that if they are really world-class philosophers then why have we not heard of them as we do hear about Richard Rorty, Jürgen Habermas and other western intellectuals. I realized that he has a point. What is the problem? What are the underlying factors which contribute to this underrepresentation? How could one overcome the paradoxes of local publishing and global perishing? Islamism is one of the most progressive political ideologies in the 20th century which is rooted in the unique experience of non-European intellectuals with modernity. Of course, like many other ideologies one can discern different and contrasting spectrums within the parameters of Islamism which could be hard to put them under one and the same conceptual umbrella. However there is no doubt that the future of Islamicate societies is deeply intertwined with Islamism as one of the most powerful streams of thought in the Muslim and even non-Muslim world. Nonetheless it is strange to see that this political position is formulated in an academic fashion by thinkers, scholars, researchers and intellectuals who are mainly in opposition to this political position. If you look at other ideological streams of thought such as Liberalism, Conservatism, Socialism, Communism, Libertinism, Anarchism and Radicalism you will soon find out that the respective proponents of these aforementioned ideologies have meticulously carried out exegeses of their political systems on the grand scale. This is not the case with Islamism. Islamism has been represented by Liberal scholars, communist intellectuals, conservative social thinkers and libertarian sociologists who have, in fact, underrepresented Islamism through *strategies of underrepresentation*. By strategies of underrepresentation I refer to *concealment* rather than *disclosure* of the conceptual paradigm of Islamism. How are these strategies applied in academia by so-called value-neutral scholars? There are many studies on these discursive strategies which function in panoptical fashions in suppressing competing discourses but one of these strategies is what Syed Farid Alatas terms as *academic imperialism*. Here I am not going to repeat what my dear friend Syed Farid Alatas has eloquently explained but it is important to note that these strategies are not only real but even powerfully efficient (Alatas, 2003). However it should be noted that I distinguish between different streams of Islamism and it would be wrong to treat them all as a monolithic whole and then according to this misleading interpretation conclude that the era of

Islamism is over—which would allow us to assume that we have entered into a new age of Post-Islamism. This is not conceptually correct and is misleading in light of sociological observations which we can deduce from existing data in Iran and other major Muslim countries. To be more accurate, we can argue that Islamism has just begun in Muslim countries such as Uzbekistan, Tajikistan, Azerbaijan, Kirgizstan, Kazakhstan, Bosnia, Albania, North Caucasian and Tatar and Bashkir Regions (within Russian Federation), Uyghur and Muslim Regions (within China), Malaysia, Egypt, and Nigeria. Of course, we should distinguish between distinct *phases* and *faces* of Islamism in, for instance, Iran and Turkey in comparison to other parts of the Muslim World. In Iran, we cannot talk about post-Islamism as though the Islamist discourse is over and soon we should expect a new set of ideas where the role of political Islam is reduced to nil. On the contrary, we may be able to expect within the next coming decades a shift from jurisprudentialist Islamism toward a post-Jurisprudentialist system of governance where other competing interpretations of Islamism could play a more visible role. For the sake of argument, I can conceptualize various streams of Islamism into five broad categories of Jurisprudentialist Islamism (e.g. Ayatollah Khomeini); Socialist Islamism (e.g. Dr. Ali Shariati), Liberal Islamism (e.g. Mohandes Mehdi Bazargan), Democratic Islamism (e.g. Ayatollah Taleghani) and Salafist Islamism (e.g. Sheikh Bin Baz). Needless to argue that within each of these paradigms there are, at least, five or six other sub-streams and each of these ideological sub-streams demonstrate authentic diversity in regard to issues such as the role of "state," social position of "women," the state of "property," and other pivotal issues in the political context of Islamism. However, today in Iran the political actors and intellectual agents are working through ideas and ideals which are within the parameters of Islamism but the question is not how to overcome Islamism. On the contrary, the crucial question is how to change the tide in terms of democratization of Islamism which was very much present in certain streams of political Islam around the 1979 Revolution. For instance, Ayatollah Taleghani's approach to Islamism represents an alternative paradigm vis-à-vis the jurisprudentialist interpretation of Islamism. The democratic approaches toward Islamism have been marginalized during these past four decades in Iran and this marginalization has not only weakened the growth of civil society in Iran but it has had a negative impact on the political trends in the Muslim World too. In other words, a return to democratic interpretation of Islamism could not be interpreted as a move toward post-Islamism as some scholars have suggested. In my view, the present century, as far as Muslim societies are concerned, is the century of Islamism both as an ideological force and as a governing paradigm. To put it differently, the end of the Cold War is not the beginning of the Ambience World Order. On the contrary, Islamism would gain more support within Muslim countries due to the fact that it is rooted in the soil of Islam (as a revealed religion which has shaped the mind and heart of people in the vast empire of Islam for more than a millennium). However the real question is that whether Muslims are able to create unity and live with diversity within the parameters of Islamism. To put it otherwise, what kind of interpretations of Islamism could bring stability and popularity, efficiency and prosperity, security and freedom, legitimacy and inclusiveness, might and cooperation (both within and without) and so on and so forth?

In other words, to address these questions require serious engagements with Islamist discourses which have reigned supreme in the Empire of Islam for the past one hundred years. It is impossible to understand these discourses through *Eurocentric* paradigms which take liberalism, communism, socialism, conservatism or secularism as their respective points of theoretical departures in conceptualizing Islamist political trends in Iran or elsewhere. This is to argue that scholars who talk about post-Islamism have not a clear idea about the major trends in Iran and these kinds of conceptual-izations demonstrate intellectual prematurity and sociological in-sensitivity.

Where does Allama Jafari stand in relation to these categories? Before answering this question, I think it would be more construc-tive to look at Islamism as a modern school of political philosophy as this would assist us to understand the political landscape in contemporary Iran and the world of Islam in a more profound fash-ion. In my view, we should distinguish between a founder (*Moasses*) and an expositor (*shareh*) in the context of political phi-losophy as this distinction would enable us to contextualize better the political thought of Allama Jafari in relation to Islamism as a modern political stream which arose as a reaction to native despot-ism and foreign colonialism. Ayatollah Khomeini is doubtless the founder of Islamism within the paradigm of jurisprudentialism but scholars such as Morteza Muttahari, Ayatollah Beheshti, Seyyed Mohammad Baghir Sadr and even Allama Mohammad Taghi Jafari were expositors of jurisprudentialist Islamism. This is not to dis-miss their respective novel approaches to political questions but it is to emphasize the pivotal distinction which exists between a founder and an expositor within the parameters of philosophical schools. One may wonder how or where one would locate the dis-course of Ayatollah Montazeri? Should one count him as a founder in the context of jurisprudentialist Islamism or an expositor? Of course, it is undeniable that Ayatollah Montazeri underwent colos-sal intellectual transformations but it is more adequate to classify him neither as an expositor nor a founder. It would be fair to con-sider him as a co-founder of the school of jurisprudentialist Islam-ism. Needless to state that Ayatollah Montazeri became very criti-cal of politics in Iran and he revised many of his views on the political role of jurisprudence in the context of the state but, in despite of many revisions, it would be a mistake to classify him as an anti-jurisprudentialist Islamist thinker. In this work, I have discussed the political thought of Allama Jafari and attempted to demonstrate how his views are compatible with the general trends within the jurisprudentialist school of political Islam. In other words, Allama Jafari has invented a novel language in demonstrating the jurisprudentialist authority within the parameters of Islamic Republicanism as founded by Ayatollah Khomeini. This is why we have classified him as an expositor as far as political philosophy is concerned but needless to reemphasize that Allama Jafari in other domains of intellectual inquiries should be viewed as one of the most creative social theorists in 20th century.

Last but not least, I would like to dedicate this book to my Turkish colleague whom I met, but forgot his name, at the Moscow conference in 2012. By writing this book, I wanted to demonstrate that in today's Iran there are many philosophers and world-class thinkers but mainly write in Persian or Arabic. It is wrong to assume that philosophy has died in Iran since the demise of Averroes in 12th century. This is a Eurocentric historiography of philosophy and history of ideas which has been inculcated in academia and most of scholars in the Muslim world repeat these distorted stories as historical facts. We are in dire need of reinventing our heritage in a non-Eurocentric fashion. This is a heroic task but it is not impossible to achieve alternative visions of reality in a multipolar world of geopolitical coalitions where Euro-Atlantism is not the only player in the town.

Chapter One

Redrawing the Map of
Political Thought in an Islamist Era

We used to state that *actions speak louder than words* and by this proverb one attempted to make a significant point, namely what one does is more significant than what one says. This is a very important principle but I think this proverb needs to be readjusted to our digitalized time where *images* speak louder than any action or word. By saying that I would like to make a point in regard to politics within the frame of Islamism which has got a negative image in a world dominated by *Facebook, Twitter, LinkedIn,* and the empire of Google, just log in into your computer and surf into Google by typing the words of *Images of Islamism* then wait for results which will baffle you dauntingly due to the results which are thrown into your face. Men with long ugly beards and women in black chadors who seem to be very angry or young men who are burning flags on the crowded dirty streets are what one gets by googling on the internet for Islamism. Violence, suicide-bombers, guns in the hands of young boys, cruelty, bloodshed, brutality and all negative words which you may associate with aggressive behaviors are among the images that one could find on the *net.com* in relation to Islamism. In other words, in the empire of Google any search on Islamism would not yield to a positive image and there is no doubt that images speak louder than both words and actions in a world that frames reality in a digitalized fashion unsurpassed in the history of humanity. Who is responsible for this misrepresentation of political Islam? Is Islam responsible for all the ills that have occurred politically in the world of Islam? Are Muslims to be blamed for all these negativities which are associated with Islam? Is it imperialism that should be blamed for regressive policies in the Muslim world? Should one make colonialism accountable for all miseries which have brought havoc upon the world of Islam and Muslims around the globe? It is undeniable that all these factors have contributed to the current state of affairs in the Muslim world but there is more to this story than what we normally hear or come across as fundamental causes of the present political regression. The *sanctification of power*, i.e. where religion and politics get into bed—while religion sanctifies politics and politics empowers religion—is the source of decline which predates both colonialism and imperialism as modern forms of oppressions and suppressions. The other factor which predates modernity is the *domineering position of literalism* which has staved off the progress of intellect as the valid source of judgment in the public sphere. The dominant position of literalism has given birth to the *mob* as a decisive force in society at the service of autocratic rulers who have worked closely with literalist interpreters of canon, known as jurists. These three factors were enough to bring down the Empire of Islam even before their encounters with Europe. In other words, in this work, I am not going to repeat postcolonial theories which hold imperialism or colonial policies responsible for all the backward state of affairs in non-European societies. By living both in Europe, USA, China, Russia and various parts of the Muslim world I have come to realize that our problems are more rooted in our worldviews rather than products of external forces such as imperialism, colonialism or modernism.

The Islamic Revolution in Iran has enabled religion to go public (Casanova, 1994) in an unprecedented fashion but it would be a grave mistake to equate Islam with Islamism (Tibi, 2012). Of course, in the minds of lay-people these two are synonymous and the source of autocratic discourses lie in this fine distinction which goes unnoticed by people who are not theoretically-equipped to distinguish between multifaceted historical and metaphysical complexities. By the collapse of metaphysical unity which was rooted in the soil of Christianity in Europe, a *Brave New World* was born, i.e. the *Enlightenment World Order*. In the absence of a religious canopy, ideologies and different forms of "isms" emerged on European horizons which were attempts to weave deeply shattered meaning-units into a homogenous meta-narrative on par with classical religions of the antiquity. Hence in the aftermath of the French Revolution Europe was turned into the hotbeds of different ideologies such as Liberalism, Democratism, Socialism, Conservatism, Anarchism, Syndicalism, Radicalism, Communism, Communitarianism, Nationalism, Individualism, Libertarianism, Anarcho-Syndicalism, and so on and so forth. By Europeanization of the world all non-European traditions came to redefine their respective intellectual/religious/political/philosophical systems in reference to the Eurocentric vision of the world, reality and being. When Europeans encountered other cultures/societies/civilizations/religions depending on the respective levels of their civilizations they were influenced by Europe in one way or the other. Less complex cultures were assimilated into European forms of life (e.g. conversion into Christianity; adoption of English or French as their new lingua franca; submission of their lands to the Whites ...) while complex or highly complex cultures became either integrated or alienated from the Eurocentric vision of the world order. By looking at the map of the Muslim world it soon becomes clear that highly complex areas of the Muslim lands could not choose either the path of assimilation or integration. On the contrary, the path of alienation or confrontation was doomed to happen as inherent forces which make up a living civilization/culture in places such as Iran or Turkey (and China as a non-Muslim as well as non-European highly complex case) would not disappear without confrontation or all-out engagement. The Islamic Revolution of 1979 was a complete rejection of the Eurocentric project which led to Europeanization of the entire gamut of the globe. But it would be a mistake to equate Europeanization project and modernity as the latter was consciously or unconsciously welcomed by many Islamists in Iran and elsewhere around the Muslim world. The majority of Iranians who took to the streets around the Revolution of 1979 were not supporters of European models of sociopolitical systems such as Communism, Liberalism, Socialism or alike but simultaneously they seemed unhappy about religious figures who chose the path of quietism too. In other words, the Eurocentric vision of politics was rejected but traditional models of religiosity did not fare very well either in contemporary political contexts which gave birth to Islamist sentiments. On the contrary, a new discourse was born but it took time to get a proper name like many other social and religious movements in the long history of humanity. To put it otherwise, similar to the French context religious unity disappeared altogether but this anomic state of affairs could not last forever. Thus a new man-made cult was born and that came to be called as ideology or *Maktab*. This novel discourse in Iran came to be known as Islamism or *Maktab Islam*. Many still think that this is equal or synonymous to Islam but this is only a solipsist illusion. Islamism is a modern ideology which has been constructed on modern basis by serving the new "church" that is called "state." There is no doubt that the future of the Muslim world belongs to Islamism and all other forms of governance (Royalism, Autocracy, ...) are doomed to disappear, but the burning question is what form of Islamism is desirable and more in tune with democratic spirit of social organization?

Among many Iranian scholars (and by extension many thinkers in the Muslim world) there is a xenophobic attitude towards the West. But this phobia has been clad under the mantle of a literalist religiosity and religious Puritanism which makes it a hard nut to crack. Since the early days of encounter between Iran and Europe majority of Iranian intellectuals attempted to distinguish between European science-technology and ideologies by arguing that the former is of universal character (i.e. welcome) and the latter of local nature (i.e. unwelcome). In other words, in overcoming *historical lag* many of intellectuals and religious scholars encouraged kings and governments to transfer science and technology from Europe but beware of ideological contamination which has to do with value-sphere. However it was not clear if all aspects of values embedded in western philosophical and intellectual traditions were of parochial nature, on the one hand, and, on the other hand, it is argued that it is not settled whether aspects of presumed universal science and technology are universal as a matter of fact. In other words, science as a model of knowledge is a matter of controversy due to its context-relatedness which reduces its position from being universal into a global paradigm of knowledge rather than a universal epistemic order. To put it differently, it is argued that science as a paradigm is a particular vision of reality and it would be a grave mistake to equate it with knowledge in its universal sense. On the other hand, it is not certain that all aspects of western philosophical traditions are of "occidental" character due to the fact that reason (and even to a higher degree intellect) are not either oriental or occidental in nature. To put it otherwise, human intellect is a universal faculty which is neither western nor eastern but while rooted in the soil of society it transcends all forms of contingencies. Having said this, I would like to argue that all that is western should not be considered as parochial or irrelevant for us or vice versa, i.e. all that is eastern should not be considered as relevant. This is to argue that all these ideological traditions are human endeavors for organizing human society in accordance to accumulated human wisdom (based on experiences on the earth) and reason as well as intellect. If this argument is valid then easternness or westernness cannot stand as the criteria of acceptance or refusal. Moreover all ideological or philosophical streams in Europe or West are not of similar origins or orientations. On the contrary, the differences between them are serious and any attempt to reduce them into insignificant differences is epistemologically mistaken. For instance, in 18th and 19th centuries, one can witness that not necessarily all socialists were democrats or all liberals considered democracy as a blessing. There are ample evidences which show how they fought against each other and used all their political muscles in destroying democracy or democratically-inspired traditions. Because, democracy is based on a universal principle which is rooted in the soil of all axial religions, i.e. a doctrine of social equality or the right of all people to participate equally in the running of their own society. Liberalism as an ideology was against this egalitarian political orientation as the culture of liberalism favored capitalism represented by the bourgeoisie over against people who were uprooted peasants (as a new labor force). Socialism as a more progressive ideology did not favor democratic principle either due to its own utopian ideals which resulted in Leninism, Stalinism, Maoism or the Soviet style of governance or Communist style of etatist ideology in China. In other words, it took more than a century for Europeans to realize that egalitarian principle is of inalienable importance in running the affairs of society as without institutionalizing this principle the state shall become either totalitarian or run the risk of being hijacked by tyrannical politicians. To put it differently, the source of power is people and they are its sole legitimator which should be realized through consensus. Now in Iran (and the Muslim world) Islamism is faced with these dilemmas, i.e. to accept democracy as a universal principle or shut it down on the basis of being a western ideal and against "our religion," "our tradition," "our national character," or "our heritage." In my view, these are excuses for those in power who do not desire to share it with people and in doing so they attempt to escape accountability and transparency. Islamism is one of the most progressive ideologies in the Muslim world provided it is interpreted within the frame of democratic spirit. Otherwise, it would turn into one of the most despotic ruling systems due to its relation with Islam as a meaning-system which is claimed to be of revealed origin. In other words, other forms of governance such as monarchism, royalism, autocracy, dictatorship and military junta are not ideal options before Muslims who insist on having *visible religiosity* in the public sphere.

However the burning question is why Islamist scholars cannot overcome these dilemmas in despite of their liberational theological stances. In other words, why do revolutionary thinkers of Islamist orientation tend to become autocratic rulers or choose to support autocratic policies under the banner of Islamic State? What are the fundamental reasons which turn Islamist activists and scholars who mostly have been struggling against tyrannical monarchies, despotic rulers, and other oppressive forms of governments into ardent supporters of totalitarianism? I think by turning to politics in order to explain political dead-ends in the Iranian context or even the context of the Muslim world we may not reach a substantive conclusion as our political problems are not solely of political nature. If they were solely of political nature then the overthrown of Pahlavi dynasty would have changed the problem of despotism but it did not. On the contrary, the repressive forms of governance were not removed by the removal of the Pahlavi dynasty but it become more complex and the Iranian social life in its totality came under the *panoptical surveillance* of the post-revolutionary state machinery which is equipped by an ideological apparatus—that is able to condition masses even internally. In other words, what was transformed by the revolution was the political regime but the autocratic culture has not been transformed yet. The question which needs to be analyzed is not of political nature, but the culture of politics in Iran (and the Muslim World) should be scrutinized if we desire to overcome autocracy. To put it differently, Islamism as a progressive political ideology needs to have a frame and that frame is the cultural context which has shaped the fabric of Iranian society for the past five thousand years. By removing Monarchism the revolutionaries were not successful in removing the autocratic cultural elements which made despotism possible in Iran for such a long time. The Islamist thinkers and scholars brought novel approaches onto the political landscape due to their engagements with socialism, modernist trends, liberalism and other novel approaches of modernity but they did not succeed in transforming the cultural mores of Iranians. To change the cultural mores we need more time and it is not certain that they could be transformed very easily. On the contrary, there are plenty of evidences that cultural mores resist over against transformational forces. The overthrown of monarchy created a political space where Islamism took the state power but soon autocratic interpretations pushed democratic inclinations to the margins under the pretexts of puritanism, jurisprudentialism and other undemocratic inclinations which only served the *culture of intolerance* and *autocracy*.

Autocracy is not only a political model of government but a cultural pattern which is deep-rooted in the Iranian society. One of its aggressive expressions is an intolerance mode of being at the individual level and despotism is the social expression at the political level. This is not confined solely to the sociopolitical level but intolerance and autocracy creep into all corners of human life and shape contours of culture. In Iran, religion plays a pivotal role as the collective unconsciousness of Iranians is conditioned by mythological and theological indices. This is not confined to Iranians alone but encompasses the entirety of the Empire of Islam in all three continents of Asia, Africa and Europe. If there is a grain of truth in my claim then one could argue that religiosity as a mode of being is deeply conditioned by mythological or theological modality. This could, in turn, mean the minimal role of reason in matters of religion. If religion was confined to esoteric dimensions of human life one could be less worried about its consequences but religion has become ideologized and as such has taken a managerial position in Iran. In other words, whenever reason is not taken seriously then other forms of categorizations may take the lead in human society. In the absence of reason authoritarian models of religiosity could be more instrumental in shaping cultural practices as emancipative types could thrive in climates where tolerance reigns supreme. This is to argue that actors do consider themselves on the side of *Truth* while condemn others as adherents of *Falsity*. This dualistic approach to reality is part and parcel of mythological/ theological visions of reality and has influenced the multifaceted patterns of scientific ethos too. To put it differently, religion in the context of the Muslim world has been interpreted within authoritarian paradigms which have not only created intolerant cultural patterns but also autocratic political institutions. The birth of Islamism in Iran has not changed these deep-rooted forms of life as revolutions tend, in despite of their claims, to change regimes of governance rather than cultures of governance. Cultural transformations may take centuries to occur unless revolutionaries are conscious about historical contingencies which have inhabited within patterns of mores, habits, attitudes, and other invisible dimensions of culture. Then one may see different productive approaches in things that matter for the improvement of human life. Literalism and legalism have silenced the gentle voice of reason in regard to religion which is used in its ideological form as a meta-narrative. Any critique of literalism is silenced culturally (and since the inception of Islamism even politically) under the legalistic pretext of violation of alleged principle of *divine boundaries*. What is the way out of this quagmire?

Religion is an ethics of being but when it is turned into politics of being then many other factors come into play which overshadows the spirit of religion as revelation. Historically religions have fallen in the hands of kings and rulers who run empires and now use them for security of their respective states or safeguarding what is termed as *national identity*. I agree that religions could produce these side-effects but these are only by-products of religion and should be treated as such. If these are taken as *raison de'etre* of religion as such then we are not talking about religion as a *covenant* between humanity and God anymore. On the contrary, we are faced by new forms of social organizations which could be either useful or harmful. Islamism is premised upon religion as a form of social organization and as such is far from being a paradigm which is concerned about *ethics of being*. It is simply a form of politics. However it is born in an autocratic form of culture which could breed counterproductive forms of life provided Islamist scholars realize that "autocracy is not the true spirit of 'our religion.'" On the contrary, the authentic spirit of "our religion" could be egalitarian form of social organization which should be established through *consensus*. Otherwise Islamism would turn into another form of despotism as various forms of monarchism turned into despotic form of governance, even the monarchs were initially supposed to be shepherds who lead their herds from various forms of perils, risks, dangers and hazards.

Islamism has played different religio-political games since its inception in Iran but three salient forms of Islamism are discernible in the public sphere. The primary form of Islamism is the form where jurisprudential approach to Islamism is not accepted on the basis of radical republicanism which cherishes egalitarian principles as sacred and unchangeable. The second form of Islamism is where jurisprudentialism or authority of jurist is acceptable as the cornerstone of political Islam with a Shiite orientation but its legitimacy is assessed democratically, i.e. through public consensus. In other words, the authority of jurist is not endowed by God but obtained through people's support which gives birth to legitimacy as an inalienable element in the constitution of political body. The third type is theocratic jurisprudentialist Islamism where the jurist is not elected by and approved by people but dis-covered by people while appointed mysteriously by the "Axis of God," i.e. the Hidden Imam in the Shiite Tradition.

Since the early days of the Islamic Revolution in Iran, one can discern these three paradigms of politics in the context of governmentality of the state apparatus. The egalitarian approach to Islamism represented by thinkers such as Ayatollah Seyyed Mahmud Taleghani was soon marginalized and excommunicated while the other two positions have employed the state for their respective purposes alternately. Today in Iran the second and third positions are known respectively as Left and Right of the position of Imam Khomeini. The Left Khomeinism seems to believe in reformism within the parameters of Islamism while the Right Khomeinism rejects reformism as counterrevolutionary act directed by imperial and colonial forces. Of course, it would be misleading to see these positions in a monolithic fashion as they are more of a multifaceted nature which could be best understood in terms of a wide conflicting spectrum. The leader of Left khomeinists is Seyyed Mohammad Khatami and the well-known ideologue of Right khomeinists is Mohammad Taghi Mesbah Yazdi. Needless to argue that there are extremist trends within the Iranian body of Islamism which are similar to Talibanism in the Sunni world but they have not yet earned public support—even after 8years of Ahmadinejad's ruthless rule.

Where should one position Ayatollah Khamenei and Ayatollah Rafsanjani in this panoramic political *landschaft*? There are many who would consider Ayatollah Khamenei as *utopian and* Ayatollah Rafsanjani as a *pragmatist* but the records speak a different language. In other words, it is too early to judge their respective legacies as they are still both unfolding novel dimensions in their political statecraft and stagecraft. To put it differently, they both demonstrate dynamism within the Shiite political traditions which shall put their indelible imprints on the future landscape of Shiism in its comprehensive fashion. The political thought of Sunni Islam has been frozen due to autocratic rule of the dynastical kingdoms in most Arab countries and in the non-Arab countries; in Turkey we may witness a novel model of Sunni political thought which may inspire Sunni Muslims in the next coming decades and even century.

What happens if Islamism becomes more democratized as a political ideology? The first thing that may occur is that we could hope that Islamism abides by the rule of the game, i.e. it respects democratic principles in managing society. In other words, it submits itself to the ballets rather than bullets, namely the decision is made through public opinion rather than coercive policies or ideologization of public discourses which attempt to equate Islam with Islam*ism*. Needless to argue that these two terms may seem very similar but one should be conscious that the role of the "ism" is not of a minor significance. On the contrary, Political Islam is a novel fashion of appropriating religion in the public sphere which does not necessarily mean a negative or a positive approach per se. What may make this appropriation a negative move depends on how democratic or undemocratic the policies are crafted in the running of the state. In other words, within the current world-system all countries and all civilizations have employed some kind of ideology for their respective states but the success and failure of each state is measured by the opinion of their respective constituencies (i.e. nation). More egalitarian societies will be more powerful in the 21st century and doubtless they shall manage world politics in the truest sense of the term. For the Muslim World the new century will be the century of Islamism and any political movement which attempts to overthrow this trend it will surely suffer badly as Muslims seem to favor *visible religiosity* in contrast to Russian, Chinese or Euro-Atlantic societies where religion is conceived differently and people seem to favor *invisible religiosity*.

Chapter Two

Governmentality in the Balance of Gnosticism

INTRODUCTION

Gnosticism by definition is a matter of *individual* significance and as such in contrast to *publicity*. On the other hand, governmentality is a collective problem and as such could not be reduced to an individual level of conceptualization. In other words, when one speaks of Gnosticism within the context of disciplinary rationality inadvertently one is referring to the most sublime dimensions of human individuality which, by definition, should not be synonymous to communal issues of public significance. However, this individualistic conceptualization of Gnosticism seems to differ from what Allama Jafari along with many other contemporary juristically-oriented thinkers in Iran refer to as *Irfan* which by definition should not lead the gnostic into seclusion or anti-social behaviors. To put it differently, if one thinks outside the Eurocentric frame of reference then the juxtaposition of governmentality and Gnosticism should not come as a surprise. Of course, this is not to argue that their combination is unproblematic or without theoretical paradoxicality. On the contrary, the nature of politics in Iran seems to suggest that certain unsurpassable challenges before politicians, who work within theoretical frame of jurists/philosophers of Shiite inclinations, are connected with admixture of Gnosticism and Politics in an unharmonious fashion. Now we have chosen Allama Jafari as an excellent example of this discourse which could assist us to shed light on contemporary paradoxes that have enveloped the public questions in Iran today.

ON MANAGEMENT AND LEADERSHIP

Allama Jafari divides leadership into two parts: 1) a leadership which is under the guidance of constructive gnosis and 2) a leadership which is dominated by mundane goals. He argues that along the tumultuous course of human history societies have oscillated between the two diametrical poles of these two kinds of leadership (2013. 278). In understanding the rationale behind this classification one needs to probe into Allama Jafari's conceptual framework in relation to constructive gnosis and what he meant by this concept. In other words, what are the characteristics of the constructive gnosis which adherence to its principles could transform the vista of governance from "mundane governance" that is under the impact of mundane goals? Here one could realize that Allama Jafari's perspective on the field of politics is not of a *political scientist* but he tends to view political landscape from the vista of a *political philosopher* or to be more accurate a *political jurist*. This inclination is discernible as he approaches politics and comparative political inquiries through a *normative prism* without taking into consideration *existing political forms* or *existing political systems*. Possibly one may ask on what grounds we have claimed in this fashion. To put it differently; why do we, firstly, assume that Allama Jafari has undertaken a comparative study and secondly on what grounds do we take for granted that his comparative inquiry is of a normative style? These questions seem not to be very difficult to answer as Allama Jafari approaches the question of politics in a dualistic fashion by arguing that there is an essential distinction between *intelligible management* and *mundane management* in the field of politics.

ON LEADERSHIP AND CONSTRUCTIVE GNOSIS

Allama Jafari states that the one who holds the office of leadership in the Islamic society must have realized the spirit of Islamic Mysticism in his own heart and mind as the principle of leadership is premised upon the notion of *mediation* between God and Humanity (2013. 278). Here it seems that Allama Jafari is endorsing the *mediative perspective* in the fields of social management and politics. One could problematize this perspective by arguing that whether this mediative political outlook may lead to some kind of authoritarian system of political organization.

Allama Jafari claims that

> due to the fact that the leader has a unique position within society then he should have himself reached a certain level of elevating growth which we term as intelligible life .... In other words, as the leader should incorporate the parameters of intelligible life in his own being due to the fact that he should, in turn, inspire the others to follow to the path of intelligible life .... However one should know that the intelligible life must be founded upon constructive mysticism as without this social life would be in danger of losing its purposeful growth. (Jafari, 2013. 278)

In this assumption endorsed by Allama Jafari one very subtle point seems to be neglected and that is the role of "state" or government as a political institution which is a modern problem and as such could transform the debate on leadership or governmentality which, in Allama Jafari's view, seems to be reduced into an individual plane. In other words, if the principle of leadership is founded upon the assumption of "mediation" between God and Humanity and based on this supposition one would take for granted that leadership is premised upon *elevation* and *excellence,* then it is clear that the intricate terrain of modern politics is not realized in a profound fashion. This could be explained in another fashion, i.e. in the context of modern nation-state the question is not one of the leadership but governmentality and this entail a very significant consequence for the whole debate of politics which seems to be missing in Allama Jafari's political discourse. In other words, in the modern context of politics which is surrounded around the idea of nation-state the crucial axis is not reducible to an individual but a system which is multilayered, multifaceted and multidimensional. Once this distinction is realized and understood fully then another problem arises before political vista of Allama Jafari which is based upon politics of leadership that is reducible to the politics of individual quality or individual-centered. The problem is if the excellent quality of this mediative perspective is not fulfilled then what should people do or how could the system check and balance the disqualified leadership?

FUNDAMENTAL OBLIGATION OF GOVERNMENT

Allama Jafari has discussed the importance of *obligation* in the field of management which seems not to be about "management" in its formal sense. On the contrary, it seems he employs the concept of "management" in the sense of "government" which is common in the parlance of politics. This is a subtle issue which should be taken into consideration as its negligence may give rise to various kinds of misunderstandings. Another issue is that Allama Jafari believes

> the most indispensable obligation of ... a leader in the Islamic
> society is ... that he ... raises the level of their awareness ... so
> they will pursue their social activities consciously and embark

upon their path freely ... as this would safeguard their social prosperity and lead them towards felicity. (2013. 278)

There are two important points here which one should take into consideration in a very profound fashion. The primary one is the concept of *felicity* which Allama Jafari regards as the pivotal axle of society and also believes that the leader should make people conscious about the true essence of felicity so they realize what constitutes the basic elements of a felicitous life. Here it looks like that Allama Jafari does not show any fundamental interest in novel democratic discourses and additionally one could read between lines that he is in favor of a normative (or even ideological) reconstruction of social order which the leadership should be founded upon that specific normative form of governmentality. The second issue is the concept of *consciousness* which Allama Jafari cherishes very deeply. His insistence upon the constitutive role of consciousness raises more questions rather than solving existing problems. In other words, what kind of consciousness does Allama Jafari think of? Is this consciousness of a political nature? Is this consciousness of a social, mental or spiritual nature? Opening up these questions lead us to the third problem in Allama Jafari's discussion, i.e. the question of freedom. When he talks about freedom one should ask what kind of freedom is Allama Jafari referring to? Is there any distinction between freedom and liberty in his political discourse? Does his conceptualization attentive to the distinction between *institutional freedom* and *spiritual freedom*? To my understanding, it seems Allama Jafari by founding leadership and social order upon *felicity* inadvertently moving towards systematic negligence of institutional freedom which encompasses civil social rights and political freedoms which could only be safeguard if we take civil rights seriously and vigilantly. One may suggest that when Allama Jafari is talking about freedom he refers to deliverance from the bondages of lust and passions (in broadest sense of both lust and passion).

LEADERSHIP AND SOCIETY

Allama Jafari approaches the question of leadership in an interesting fashion which reads as follow

> in fact, within each of us there is a compass which demonstrates
> to each of us the most felicitous state of being in the gamut of
> reality .... The duty of a leader is to pave the ground for realiza-
> tion of such state of being and allow the society to embark upon
> this felicitous path as ... in the absence of freedom people may
> drift away from good life ... which is based on blissful gnosis.
> (2013. 279)

In this statement one can discern that Allama Jafari assumes that
the leader is someone who should be equipped with the highest
form of consciousness and has also reached the most elevated form
of awareness which would enable him to provide the necessary
conditions for realization of the *intelligible life*—so people in the
society could embark upon a purposeful life in the world of being.
This, in my view, is a very delicate issue which intellectuals and
philosophers should dwell upon, but my question here is of another
order. In other words, if the leader did not prepare the necessary
conditions for people, or even worse, he attempted to obstruct the
emergence and institutionalization of the *intelligible life* in society,
then what should people do? I gather the problem in the Jafarian
discourse lies within his unit of analysis which is not the "social"
but the "existence." In other words, Allama Jafari explicates in a
very remarkable fashion the context of awareness in relation to
existence but he does not elaborate the social factors which are
instrumental in creating such awareness in a political system. This
is to state that Allama Jafari conceptualizes the necessary conditions in an ideal state but neglects the actual context which we live
in.

GOVERNING AND ALIENATION

The question of alienation is one of the key problems in philosophy, human sciences and theology. Allama Jafari has brought this issue into philosophy of politics and engaged on relevant issues in regard to alienation based on an Islamic perspective. He argues that contemporary humanity is afflicted with an incurable "dis-ease" of machinism which has turned humanity into *unconscious thing*. Needless to state that Allama Jafari does not settle for a purposeless criticism of present state of affairs, but, on the contrary, he takes a step further by creating an alternative for *current global order* which in his view is the only *path of deliverance* before humanity today. In other words,

> based on a comprehensive approach towards religious sources ... and through a normative knowledge of human being ... one can conclude that ... the governor or the governing body ... which takes the responsibility to manage people in a society ... in fact ... resembles a sane and full-grown person ... who knows and manages his own body members in the best possible fashion. Establishing this kind of relationship ... between the managing or governing body ... and the constituting members of the society ... which are acting under the dominance of the managing body ... is the most appropriate and logical relationship which one can conceive between the rulers and the ruled. It is based on this style of government or management which people ... could put themselves ... freely at the disposal of the governing body or management .... Any ... other style of management or government is not worth to be considered as humane ... managing configuration. I would rather consider it as the management of bees in the society of beehives. (2013. 280)

Here there are two issues which I think are important to note. The first issue is related to the conceptual framework of Allama Jafari, where the latter employs two concepts in relation to politics in a particular fashion which are not common in discursive disciplines today. The first one is the concept of "the person of manager" and the second one is "the office of management." In the translation I have tried to use more accessible concepts of "governor" and "governing body" so the English reader will not get confused and lost in translation. However, the matter of fact remains to be discussed is not solely of etymological nature but of political significance. In other words, at first instance, it may seem that Allama Jafari's conceptualization is of an exceptional caliber as in religious sources within Shiite traditions in relation to political jurisprudence and political philosophy very rarely one talks about the governor as a "manager." Of course, one cannot deny that managing the affairs of a society is ascribed implicitly to the governor which brings to mind the concept of management again. However, when within contemporary Persian one uses terms such as "Modir" or "Modiriyat" then they are not equivalent to *governor* and *government*. On the contrary, the first one refers to *manager* and the second term is equivalent to *management* in English parlance. If these observations are correct then a question could be raised by a critical reader who takes the political discourse of Allama Jafari in a serious fashion. The blunt question is what does Allama Jafari mean by "Manager" and "Management Office" in the context of politics?

If this question could be of any epistemological merit then I think we are about to enter one of the most thorny terrains within contemporary political thought in Iranian traditions of Islamism. In other words, any answer to this question would not be solely confined to Allama Jafari's political paradigm but, in fact, whole new questions and paradigms and thinkers should be reconceptualized in the light of Democratic Islamism. I think due to the paradigmatic similarities which exist between discourses of Ayatollah Beheshti, Ustad Muttahari and even Doctor Shariati and Allama Jafari one could guess what the latter intended by the "Person of Manager" and the "Office of Management." In other words, the former seems to refer to *jurist* and the latter to *jurisprudential authority*. If this reading of Allama Jafari's discourse could be rated as appropriate then another question may arise and that is why did he re-construct the contemporary jurisprudential concepts which have been deeply institutionalized in the Iranian body politic as well as upheld as the ideological apparatus of the present Islamic State?

The second issue is related to Allama Jafari's claim on the alienated state of contemporary humanity. He believes that the contemporary self is inflicted with an incurable disease of alienation and its root lies within the *form* or *style* of capitalist system of governance which does not provide us with any sense of salvation unless we concede to *Islamic Managing Style*, i.e. the political system where the relation between the governor and the governed is akin to that of "I" and "Body Members." My question is whether this type of management is the only way of redeeming humanity from alienated existence and/or has this fashion of political administration itself obstructed the full emergence of functioning civil society in Iran. This is a subtle issue which Allama Jafari glosses over in a rapid manner without mentioning it anywhere in his writings. In other words, when the unit of analysis is the "world," "life," or "existence" rather than being the "social" then a very peculiar accident occurs and that is the disappearance of "context" from analyses. This is evident in Allama Jafari's discourses on politics in a very noteworthy fashion. To put it otherwise; in his framework of political analysis there is barely any reference to concrete events which have transformed the Iranian political landscape such as the Constitutional Revolution, the Nationalization Movement of Iranian Oil, Islamic Revolution of 1979 and many other contemporary events which without one cannot fathom politics and its consequences both locally and globally.

MANAGEMENT'S FUNDAMENTAL OBLIGATION

Allama Jafari dedicates a very long section in his *Islamic Mysticism* on *manager's obligation in Islamic system* which is of great interest for understanding the conceptual universe of contemporary political Islamism in Iran and its structural impact on the fabric of political system in today's Iran. He argues that

> *the management body in a society should care for people who are within their territory ... by realizing and also ... accepting the fact that the being of humanity is consisted of two dimensions ... i.e. material and spiritual. In addition, one should not neglect the importance of a crucial fact in regard to managing of human society... namely the pivotal superiority of spiritual dimension over against the material aspect .... In other words, thanks to the ultimate purpose of life which is ... to be under guardianship of the divine light ... so the managing body in the society should realize the importance of the spiritual dimension and make sincere efforts in actualizing the necessary conditions for people to reach to that level of God-consciousness.* (2013. 282)

I think this is a good idea. As a matter of fact, when one reads the political discourses of Islamism since early 50s in the twentieth century one comes frequently across great ideas and ideals which were inspired by a leftist fervor but directed against both the capitalist and socialist camps. For instance, Ayatollah Taleghani was one of the ardent critics of Capitalism but this did not mean that he was in favor of Socialism. On the contrary, he rebuked communist system of governance in the Soviet Union but kept philosophical distance from the capitalist discourses of liberalism and other schools of thought both in philosophy and economics. However these critical discourses within Islamism did not have any clear idea about the institutionalization phase which came after the establishment of the Islamic Revolution in 1979. For instance, Ayatollah Taleghani critiqued both liberal as well as the socialist discourses in regard to "social justice" by arguing that quantitative justice (Adl) is not enough in realizing the best possibilities of human being in any society. In other words, he argues for a qualitative justice (Ghest) which could overcome the deficiencies of both systems of governance by paving the way for humanity to enter a new era. Needless to argue that the emergence of the Islamic State has demonstrated a different scenario where the system has collected the deficiencies of the capitalist as well as the socialist models without being able to produce a distinct system in areas of culture, economy, politics, and other relevant domains of social life. If these remarks are of any significant then I would dare to take a step further and argue that this *idealist syndrome* is not specific to Taleghani but includes all Islamist intellectuals and writers of the 20th century in Iran (and even the entire world wherever Islam has entered into political frame of reference). In other words, when Allama Jafari discusses the fundamental obligation of managing body the first question which comes to mind is not about how we could improve the spirituality within the public discourse of politics in Iran. On the contrary, the main problem is if the governor or managing body of politics within an Islamic society did not fulfill their duty then in what fashion could people make them accountable? To put it differently; what are the mechanisms of accountability within an Islamist political system? It seems within the political philosophy and political sociology of Allama Jafari there is no roadmap for solving these kinds of political questions. One could mention thousands reasons for Allama Jafari's negligence in this regard but that is not my concern here as I am trying to find out the underlying ideas within Iranian political traditions which have obstructed the emergence of an accountable political system in contemporary Iran. Some argue that the undemocratic character of politics in Iran is due to Islam or the current leadership of Iranian politics as the revolutionaries before the Iranian Revolution in 1979 convinced the public that the Old Regime is responsible for all the ills in Iran and Islam is the sole panacea for all deadlocks which Iran was facing. But the historical events after the establishment of the ideals of Revolution proved that these kinds of arguments are unsubstantiated and wrong. The political problems in Iran are of intellectual nature rather than political.

THE INTELLIGIBLE LIFE AND EQUAL RIGHTS

Allama Jafari has dedicated a great deal of his works on human existence within the parameters of intelligibleness. As a matter of fact within his numerous publications we can find an important treatise which is entitled *intelligible life*. In his *Islamic Mysticism* he talks also about life within the parameters of intelligibleness and equality in regard to human rights which is the foundation of felicity as well as sought-after by people of all walks of life. This interesting topic has compelled him to embark upon a comparative research in the field of management. Allama Jafari argues that the western managing framework is deficient and suffers from an incomplete vision of human reality. He explains that

> ... when we speak of intelligible life and its relation to the felicity ... this is not only meant for governing or managing elite in a particular society ... and those who are in the lower ladders of society should be excluded from a decent and humane form of life .... I deeply disagree with thinkers such as Fredrick Winslow Taylor who reduces the existential capacity of ordinary people ... such as working classes ... in the society to the level of an ... intelligent gorilla .... Is this not an insult and assault to human dignity and honor? (2013. 283)

In my reading of Allama Jafari in this context there seems to be an issue which subtlety has been put in abeyance. If we exclude the Taylor who lived in the capitalist society of the United States of America where people may not be concerned to be *under the attracting ray of divine light*—then a serious question could arise about the so-called Islamic society where the Islamic state tends to ignore human beings in a dramatic fashion by not considering them even at the level of a gorilla—let alone an *intelligible gorilla*. Thus what should be done under these kinds of circumstances? In other words, what are the controlling mechanisms at the disposal of people by which they can make the leader (and the leadership body of politics) accountable in an Islamic state? By critiquing history, the West, and the "other," it seems Allama Jafari leaves substantial political issues unsaid which could have assisted the democratic movement in Iran (and even contributed to the larger Muslim World). By taking the West as the chief other, Allama Jafari has ignored the *political context of Iran* in a fashion that his critiques leave us in a limbo situation as one does not know what should be done about the undemocratic nature of politics in contemporary Iran. Why should one in Iran be so much concerned about the political state of America rather than rectifying the loopholes in the Iranian system?

Apart from this critique one should realize that in Taylor's discourse there is no implicit similarity between "government" and "management" as one comes across in Allama Jafari's paradigm. Once we realize this point then we may be right to assume that Allama Jafari has critiqued Taylor on wrong assumptions as the latter was not concerned about management in the sense of governing but he was exactly interested in methods of improving workforce in specific industrial organizational contexts. To put it differently; Taylor sought to improve industrial efficiency. Taylor, as the father of scientific management, was arguing that the work as a phenomenon deserves to be approached by a systematic observation. The context of his notion of management is as important as the subject of his research, i.e. the industrialized society which has created the working masses in the developed countries in an unparallel fashion. By looking at the key principles of Taylor's scientific management one could realize that Allama Jafari did not understand the context of Taylorian discourse as it is consisted of four principles:

1. Replace rule-of-thumb work methods with methods based on a scientific study of the tasks.
2. Scientifically select, train, and develop each employee rather than passively leaving them to train themselves.
3. Provide detailed instruction and supervision of each worker in the performance of that worker's discrete task.
4. Divide work nearly equally between managers and workers, so that the managers apply scientific management principles to planning the work and the workers actually perform the tasks. (Drucker, 1974)

One of the grave mistakes of Allama Jafari's dialog with western thinkers and on occidental discourses is his lack of sensitivity towards the question of *context* as though thought and ideas appear in a vacuum without any relation to historical contexts and settings. Here we see very clearly that Taylor is approaching the question of management in an industrial context in the capitalist setting of early 20th century but Allama Jafari redefines management in its disciplinary meaning and instead talks about government and the ills of western reductionism in regard to human personality. This is not arguing for institutionalized reductionism which reigns over in western scientific ethos but as Rumi once said "If you don't respect the hierarchical order then it is justified to be blamed for heresy." In this context it seems Allama Jafari has taken the concept of "intelligible gorilla" out of its proper setting without being concerned about the full picture which was related to improving the workforces in an industrial system. Of course, the work of Taylor has been critiqued by various management theorists since its early emergence. Management theorist Henry Mintzberg is, for instance, highly critical of Taylor's methods. Mintzberg states that an obsession with efficiency allows measureable benefits to overshadow less quantifiable social benefits completely, and social values get left behind (1989. 333).

Last but not least, if we are allowed to consider Allama Jafari's critique of Taylor relevant then that should be in relation to intensification of workers' alienating state of existence which was brought up by socialist thinkers who challenged Taylor's methods of transferring control over production from workers to management, and the division of labor into simple tasks. They argued that Taylorism intensified the alienation of workers that had begun with the factory system of production around 1870–1890. But again on this account I don't see any relation between management in Taylorian discourse and government of society which Allama Jafari seems to be concerned about.

Chapter Three

Religion, Politics, and Other Sagas

INTRODUCTION

One of the most perplexing problems within social and human sciences is the question of the "other." To put it more accurately, one of the serious challenges before social and human scientists is how to conceptualize the "other" without running the risk of obscuring or distorting the "other." In other words, the question of understanding the "other" has been so badly misrepresented that many critics talk about "othering" and by this they refer to complex cognitive/emotional/intellectual processes which lead to distortion of the other rather than comprehension of the other (society, history, religion, intellectual tradition, nation, country…). One of the most known examples of such othering-project is Eurocentrism which has come to be critiqued for so many reasons by so many scholars from all walks of life. However, it would be a mistake to think that this act of othering is only an intellectual disease confined to European thinkers alone. On the contrary, ethno-centrism is a universal ill which could inflict any tradition or any scholar as the psychological processes which may cause processes of othering are as pivotal as other sociological and intellectual factors. To put it differently, non-western thinkers have rightly become critical of

Eurocentrism but this should not desensitize eastern scholars before ethnocentric projects or vectors which are rampant among many of us who are critical of Eurocentrism. In this chapter, we shall pay closer attention to aspects of this problem by focusing on Allama Jafari's engagements with the "other."

POLITICS: A CONCEPTUAL MAKEOVER

Politics as a concept is as old as human society itself but if we take, for instance, Greek and Iranian traditions as distinct classical points of departures then we may be able to get a rounded picture of the lexical meanings of this term which have been dramatically as well as drastically transformed both in the East and West since the ancient time. In the Greek tradition, the concept of politics referred to *polis* which literally means city, citizenship or even body of citizenship. As a concept in modern English context one could define politics as either t he activities associated with the governance of a country or area or the activities of governments concerning the political relations between different countries. But within the conceptual texture of politics in the sense of an activity both political philosophers and political scientists discern an artistic or scientific element of influencing other people on a civic or individual level. In the Iranian tradition, the concept of politics was conceptualized as siyasat. The term could be better understood when it is analyzed through its synonyms in Persian language, i.e. being sayyas or making tanbih. The word sayyas in Persian language means a deceitful person, i.e. a person who knows how to manipulate the situation or others in a very cunning fashion which would yield the maximum result for their illegitimate purposes. While the first connotation of siyasat is associated with deception and fraudulence nevertheless the second connotation, i.e. tanbih refers to a more positive picture where a humane image of this complex concept is implicitly conceived, i.e. entebah (awareness). It may be of interest to note that the word tanbih has come to be associated with physical punishment in Persian and this sense of the term could be related to the transformation of institutional character of politics in the history of Iran where the awareness aspect has lost its importance and instead other aspects have come to play more important roles due to the dominance of tribal mentalities rather than civic awareness.

Now that we have elaborated briefly the different approaches to politics in the Iranian and Greek traditions respectively, it is high time to see how Allama Jafari has conceptualized politics. In Islamic Mysticism he assigns a great deal on the role of politics and the relation between spirituality (religion/culture) and politics. He defines politics as "management and making sense of the societal life for people in the society" (Jafari, 2013. 299).

In his view, politics could not be dissociated from other domains of social life such as art, religion, morality, culture, science and so on and so forth. Any attempt to study human society without paying attention to these undeniable interconnectivities would have destructive consequences for the human psyche and human civilization in its broadest sense (Jafari, 2013. 300). Nevertheless, there is one issue which needs to be taken into consideration as Allama Jafari seems to approach politics through a jurisprudential point of departure which has come to be known as Islamism in contemporary political discourses. If this claim bears any sense of truth then one could assume that Allama Jafari is advocating some kind of theologization of politics in Iran rather than making a sociological observation about the connectivity of various human domains in society. This is a simple point but needs to be borne in mind as the loss of this distinction would create grave misunderstandings in comprehending Allama Jafari's political discourse within the context of contemporary Iranian branch of Islamism.

RELIGION: EMANCIPATIVE OR OPPRESSIVE FACTOR?

Morality and ethics in the context of modernity are issues which have engaged Allama Jafari for good part of his intellectual dialogs with western thinkers, scholars and academics. By critiquing ethics of modernity he attempted to rescue religion from being responsible before calamities, atrocities, catastrophes and various forms of oppressions which have been inflicted upon humanity. In other words, Allama Jafari claims that

> religion, mystic traditions and divine morality ... in essence, ... are responsible for ... humanity's perfectional transformation ... then ... as such they would never turn into their opposites .... In other words, religion would never turn into something negative which would stave off the path of humanity's perfectional transformation. (Jafari, 2013. 300)

By reading this view on religion, morality and divine tradition one would wonder whether this perspective is accurate or it is in dire need of being dramatically qualified. Although Allama Jafari does not refer to disciplinary debates on religion as a paradigm of liberation or emancipation but it is not farfetched to conclude that he considers the emancipative quality of religion as an essential aspect while disregarding the oppressive role of religion—particularly in the political context of Iran—by glossing over it as an accidental dimension of religion. Here we need to deconstruct the question of religion by retracing conceptual styles through which the concept of religion has been understood within the Enlightenment Tradition and contrast it with what Allama Jafari and many contemporary Islamist scholars considered as the nature of religion within the context of human civilization.

Within the paradigms of the Enlightenment Tradition key progressive scholars have conceptualized religion in terms of its oppressiveness. In other words, the oppressive dimensions of religion have been researched upon in extensive fashions. However, the liberative/emancipative role of religion has been mainly neglected or denied in the context of social movements and political revolutions. The classical example is the Iranian Revolution of 1979 which took sociologists and political scientists by an awful surprise as for quite some time many experts tried to reduce the importance of religion in the constitution of the Iranian social movement. The disciplinary lapse committed by academic sociologists and political scientists has been in another fashion mimicked by Islamist scholars who seem to neglect in toto the oppressive dimensions of religions by dogmatically insisting on positive aspects of all that is religious. Allama Jafari's approach to religion in contrast to modernity seems to belong to this category of scholarship which lacks what Rudolf J. Siebert terms critical theory of religion. Maybe Ali Shariati's approach towards religion could be more constructive rather than Allama Jafari's where the former worked through the paradigm of religion against religion, i.e. a paradigm is sensitive to both oppressive and emancipative dimensions of religion within society where opposite and apposite complex and multivariate forces are at work.

POLITICAL GNOSTICISM OR MYSTICAL POLITICS

Political Islam, after its consolidation in Iran, opted for a new strategy whereby religious rituals in Islam came to be redefined under politicized reading of religion. For instance, Friday Prayer which is one of the rituals in Islam—and less attended by Shiite Muslims in the absence of the infallible twelfth Imam—came to be redefined in a novel fashion by reconceptualizing it as politico-religious Friday Prayer. By reading Allama Jafari's reflections on political questions and religion one cannot but tend to see parallels between discourses on political Islam and Allama Jafari's problematizations on religion in relation to politics. There are ample examples in his works which support my interpretation of similarity between political Islam and Allama Jafari's political discourse. Allama Jafari divides politics into two broad categories, i.e. humane politics and inhumane politics (or what he terms as Machiavellian or Leviathan-istic political value-system). He defines humane politics as

> a particular style of management whereby people in the society are influenced in a fashion that ... aspirations towards higher ideals and worthy goals become sine qua non both in the individual and collective realms .... When politics is defined in this manner then one could argue that it is one of the greatest forms of worships for human beings .... Why is that so? Because ... without justification ... and inevitable ordering of social life ... nobody would be able to fulfill his/her ritual duties, ... realize moral duties and even enjoy the fruits of sane culture. (Jafari, 2013. 301)

This quote should be reread very carefully as one could see one of the most significant changes in theological conceptualization of Shiite political thought in the modern context of post-Imperial Iran where the new form of nation-state governance has taken shape in the Muslim World. How do I reach to this conclusion? Allama Jafari uses various prophetic traditions and canonical statements such as everybody is shepherd and all of you are responsible before subjects or if you wake up and on that day you don't care about communal problems in your society then you are not a Muslim and many other of these kinds of hadiths without being concerned that these concepts may not be compatible to political concepts which don't relate political activities to a higher order. In other words, if we wake up and don't care about the communal problems in our society and this carelessness may push us towards being without the circle of faith this does not mean necessarily that the issue is over within the modern political system as the state will punish us here and now. While in the former framework the duty is conceptu-alized in relation to the higher order and one's negligence is treated in theological sense rather than political sense. These issues apart, there is a very interesting point here which demonstrates clearly the political position of Allama Jafari which is very similar to the politics of Islamism. He argues that "one of the greatest forms of worships is political activity" (2013. 301) and he brings up plentitude of examples which could be supportive of this claim. Now one may ask whether this is not a form of power where jurisprudentially concept of authority is read into religious politics and political religion. Is this paradigmatic confluence accidental or the existing similarity between jurisprudential concept of authority and Allama Jafari's political outlook of a peripheral import which one cannot find any deep-seated conceptual interrelationships between these two discourses?

Within jurisprudential form of governance the primary importance is attached on the political dimension and all other realms are conditioned upon the discretion of jurist whose authority is an extension of the divine authority which was conferred upon the prophetic office on the Earth. In other words, this theological definition of power gives an absolute authority to the jurisprudential establishment in categorizing all that matters in human society where religion has been established as a political frame of reference. When Allama Jafari puts forward the thesis that political activity is one of the most significant forms of rituals or worships then it is almost impossible to interpret his discourse in a non-jurisprudential fashion as prior to the rise (and establishment of) Islamism there was a clear distinction between the realm of "Moamelat" and the realm of "Ebadat." These realms have been combined together in the context of Islamism and Allama Jafari has not questioned or even critically assessed the validity of this combination. It seems he has taken this blending for granted and upon this jurisprudential definition of religion he has started to build up his political edifice. That's why we consider his political project as another form of Islamism which is not compatible with a democratic reading of politics. This is not to argue that Islam is not compatible with democracy or other rational achievements as Islam is a religion and cannot be compared with cultural achievements of humanity. What is at stake here is a form of politics in the eastern countries which has come to be known as Islamism that has not taken democratic values very seriously yet. There are ample historical evident that other forms of politics such as liberalism, socialism, communism, and conservatism at their earlier stages in the 19 [th] and 20 [th] centuries were not attentive to democratic principles but gradually proponents of these respective political ideologies accepted the role of people in the running of societal affairs. The Islamic Revolution in 1979 has created an opportunity before Iranians (and even many Muslim countries) through which the proponents of Islamism should gradually move towards democratic principles of accountability, transparency, and participatory form of governance as these principles are not and cannot be against Islam. On the contrary, they are against authoritarian interpretation of Islamism which, in the first place, could be realized when the public lend their supports in 1979. Otherwise, there could never be a political movement without public support, no matter how great its ideals may appear in theory.

POWER AND ITS FUNCTIONS

One of the most complex issues in the field of politics is the problem of power and its mechanisms and functions within society. Allama Jafari approaches the question of power by arguing that

> authority and powerful ... both belong to essential attributes of God. Thus ... obtaining accurate knowledge about power and might ... leads to comprehending one of the divine attributes ....
> In other words, by realizing and employing it in a rightful manner ... one is able to further the frontiers of human self-actualization ... in the context of intelligible life ... this is to argue that by learning about authority and power as divine attributes one shall be equipped with divine manifestations which are nec-

essary in one's pursuit in life based on intelligibility. (Jafari, 2013. 304)

If we assume that Allama Jafari is of the belief that politics is the key important factor in the constitution of society as well as the founding-block in the geometry of intelligible life, then one of the most problematic questions in the context of politics may emerge which needs to be tackled in a serious fashion. In other words, the most significant problem pertinent to Allama Jafari seems to be that he views power and the emergence of intelligible life in the context of society which is considered as constituting aspects of politics— within theological frame of reference which leads him to neglect the mechanisms of authority within sociological paradigm. This inexcusable negligence has resulted in Allama Jafari's inattention towards patterns as well as complex mechanisms of power as in-controvertible aspects of governing (government, ruling and governmentality) in human societies as well as in the context of modern nation-state system—which has been amazingly aban-doned in his political discussions as though this subject is of no importance within political discourses and contemporary politics.

MANIFESTATIONS OF AUTHORITY

Allama Jafari brings up a very important question along the debates on mysticism and authority which, on the one hand, is deeply relat-ed to politics in its general sense, and, on the other hand, demon-strates his theological inclination in the field of politics. In my view, one of the most serious objections which could be leveled at the theological interpretation of Allama Jafari's political perspec-tive is his negligence of social sources of power or what it could be figuratively termed as terrestrial power which could influence dif-ferently within distinct historical contexts by generating divergent forms of authority. For instance, Allama Jafari argues that

power does not stand on the path of right as the true essence of
power is ... right par excellence ... thus it is not conceivable to
consider a false identity for power along its true essence ....
However it is undeniable that what exists is in contradiction to
this true essence of power .... In other words, the actual state of
affair is a result of ... actions of those in power who endorse
falsehood ... and use their authority in annihilating supporters of
truth and right .... If one could see the true essence of power ...
it would be readily obvious that power is one of the most sacred
manifestations of the divinity .... This holy manifestation in
the ... hands of Ali would be employed solely in reviving the
path of truth and extinguishing the fire of falsehood .... (Jafari,
2013. 304-5)

It is interesting to note that in this style of conceptualizing politics what is surprisingly absent is the fact that Allama Jafari mentions concepts such as power, authority and political realm without
any concrete reference to structure or agency. In other words, within Allama Jafari's paradigm there is no trace of contextualization of
politics which could give us a clue where he heads on. To put it
differently, in his Islamic Mysticism when Allama Jafari attempts
to conceptualize politics he starts from the divine attributes and
slowly moves to Imam Ali and his charismatic personality without
mentioning historical characteristics of Imam Ali's rule (and the
political issues, mechanisms of power in a tribal society which got
united under one faith and the beginning of a new imperial state).
On the contrary, Allama Jafari shies away from historical analysis
and glosses over sociological considerations which could assist us
in understanding significant implicit structures in the sense of political sociology. In other words, what Allama Jafari, like many other
contemporary Islamist thinkers in terms of political thought, has
done is imposing a mythic vision on politics and afterwards pursu-
ing his theological concerns in the context of politics. What is the
problem with a mythic vision of political question which is conceptualized in a theological frame of reference? I think this approach

has led to an absolutist stance in politics which has drastically affected the Iranian society in the last fifty years by transforming all corners of life in Iran (and even the Muslim World and beyond). In other words, issues such as authority, power, source of power, and many other similar concepts belong to political field which is very fluid and related to multifaceted practical realities. Once they are conceptualized in an absolutist fashion an intellectual stagnation sets in and actors in such a society feel like being chained in an iron cage. To put it more bluntly, ahistorical interpretation of political history of Islam or idealistic reading into sacred texts within the Iranian contexts only benefits authoritarian discourses in the jurisprudential political system which exerts more pressures on democratic and public-friendly interpretations of Islamism. By resorting to the idealist-cum-mythic discourse the Islamist political thinkers have not revived "sacred ideals" in the public sphere and in the hearts of people in Iran or elsewhere. On the contrary, what they have inadvertently created is the consolidation of authoritarian discourses in Iran which have suffocated democratic interpretations of Islamism where the criterion is people's vote and not intentions of absolute jurisprudential authority which is allegedly modeled upon the prophetic authority. The more we move away from actual political issues in Iran we can witness the rising intensity of an ailing idealistic discourse. This intensity is an issue which could be studied in the political discourse of Allama Jafari where power is conceptualized in terms of manifestations rather than forms of power.

When we talk about "forms of power" then this signifies that we refer to societal mechanisms which produce, create, recreate and reproduce various forms of authority within the body of politics. However when we use concepts such as the ones employed by Allama Jafari, i.e. Tajalliyat or manifestations then it is clear that we are thinking of power in theological terms which would surely influence our concepts of legitimacy and source of power by sacralizing rather than socializing the processes of political consensus.

RELIGION AND ITS JANUS-FACE

One of the central issues within humanities and social sciences is the question of religion and its relation to social changes and political transformations. In other words, how and in what fashion religions could have influenced colossal human transformations in various historical epochs and contemporary world. Needless to argue that philosophers talk usually about "Religion" but sociologists prefer to conceptualize "religion" in particular historical contexts with specific social modalities rather than religion in its universal-cum-essential sense. This is to state that religion at the level of "Umm ul-Ketab" (in its essential modality) is hard to be caught by sociologists but religion in the sense of *religious institutions* in different contexts such as *confrontation, conflict, interaction, opposition, dialog, dialectic, reciprocity, exchange,* and *interchange* with other factors such as culture, politics, economy, social, science, art, cinema, law, military, and metaphysics could become a subject of investigation. This distinction is very crucial and could assist us when analyzing the state of political thought in contemporary Iran as most often it is glossed over without realizing how significant it could be in terms of methodological considerations.

In *Islamic Mysticism* Allama Jafari discusses *The Crisis of Contemporary Culture* by engaging with the ideas of Albert Schweitzer who received the 1952 Nobel Peace Prize for his philosophy of Ehrfurcht vor dem Leben or *Reverence for Life* (Seaver, 1951). The central idea in this philosophy has been defined by James Brabazon who is the author of the *Biography of Albert Schweitzer* as *The Will to Live*, i.e. the only thing we are really sure of is that we live and want to go on living. This is something that we share with everything else that lives, from elephants to blades of grass—and, of course, every human being. So we are brothers and sisters to all living things, and owe to all of them the same care and respect, that we wish for ourselves (Brabazon, 2005).

Allama Jafari cherishes Schweitzer's critical assessment of the modern civilization by arguing that

> *some of western thinkers ... have come to agree with eastern intellectuals and Muslim philosophers* [on the critical state of contemporary culture and ... how to bring radical changes which could assist us in overcoming the crises through a revolution] .... (Jafari, 2013. 310)

Allama Jafari agrees that Schweitzer is right when the latter holds that "we are at the brink of cultural self-destruction" (Jafari, 2013. 310) and also concedes Schweitzer's position on the "necessity of revolution" (Jafari, 2013. 311) but, at the same time, he critiques Schweitzer which needs to be reflected upon very carefully. Let me quote Schweitzer on the cultural self-destruction which compels him to argue that

> it is obvious to everybody that we are in the process of cultural self-destruction. What is left is also not secure any more. It still stands because it was not exposed to the destructive pressure to which the rest has already succumbed. The only meaningful way of life is activity in the world; not activity in general but the activity of giving and caring for fellow creatures. *(Schweitzer quoted by Allama Jafari, 2013. 310-11)*

In other words, Schweitzer postulated the necessity for a Renaissance of collective life that would be organized by the spirit of solidarity and reverence for life. In this Renaissance,

> activity which is the product of reasonable deliberation ... is the fundamental principle ...; the only logical and practical principle ... for historical evolution which has been presented by human being .... I am convinced that ... if we are thoughtful people ... surely this revolution could take place .... (ibid. 312)

I needed to quote Schweitzer before engaging on Allama Jafari's view on the role of revolution which Schweitzer refers to in relation to the imminent cultural self-destruction as the conclusion which Allama Jafari draws in this regard seems to be grounded on a very shaky foundation and relevant to my concerns on religion and politics in Iran. Allama Jafari argues that

> the revolution which Schweitzer talks about regardless of its possible type ... surely it will be founded upon adjustment of selfishness/despotic tendencies/oppressive inclinations/hedonistic propensities ... but ... due to the fact that these adjustments ... could not be sustained without having recourse to religion ... then one could guess ... that the revolution which Schweitzer deliberates on ... is inevitably of religious kind ... and Islam ... and in particular the Shiite branch of Islam ... has been waiting for as the global divine government. (2013. 312)

Here we are faced with various distinctive issues which need to be carefully analyzed as it is not clear what Schweitzer mean by *Renaissance*. Apart from this, it is not clear that Allama Jafari's conclusion based on Schweitzer's vision of *imminent revolution* is accurate due to many faulty issues which make such conclusive correlations baseless. For instance, connecting revolution as a modern sociological concept to theological vision of reality which has been cherished in Shiism is a matter which needs to be corroborated and not simply stated. Another problem is that Allama Jafari states that this is Albert Schweitzer's *Noble Prize Acceptance Speech* but the lengthy quotation which Allama Jafari refers to in his debate on *the contemporary crisis of culture* is taken from Schweitzer's celebrated work, i.e. *Civilization and Ethics*. There are other significant questions which seem Allama Jafari has glossed over in a questionable fashion. The first question which arises in this context is about the very notion of "religion" which Allama Jafari works by in the context of Schweitzer's Revolution.

In other words, if we assume that a revolution is imminently upon us, which would overshadow the destiny of all human societies in the globe, and this imminent revolution is of a *religious type*, then the serious question is what interpretation or reading of religion is in mind. Because in Iran we have had the experience of a *religious revolution*, we should then be more cautious when using the term "religion" without conceptual problemization. An all-emancipative interpretation of religion, religious institutions and clergy was the result of a naïve perspective rooted in the romanticization of religion and all that is religious in an unconditional fashion in 1960s and 1970s by intellectuals in Iran. Having this modern Iranian historical experience it is harder today to be so optimistic about religion without realizing interpretative nuances or styles of readings which could condition and even alter the spirit of religion as a socio-political panacea. Moreover, it is not clear that even the very Schweitzerian notion of revolution is inevitably related to or possible to be related to question of savior in Shiism. I think each of these issues needs to be carefully conceptualized as they seem to be weaved into a single texture without organic correlation. Furthermore, it is not clear if we are permitted to generalize the concept of "revolution" into the movement of the savior as described in sacred canons and transmitted statements by the infallible figures in the Shiite tradition. I think this is a grave mistake which has inflicted the Shiite theological schools which have opted for politicized interpretations of the sacrosanct tradition. The last but not least important issue which I need to mention in this context is that despotism, tyranny, autocracy, cruelty, absolutism, and all other oppressive acts are even possible within a so-called religious state. Thus, one should be more cautious in critiquing the *other* while being so deeply self-congratulatory toward one's own self (tradition, culture ...).

Chapter Four

Social Life Redesigned

INTRODUCTION

Whenever one talks about democracy in Iran and many other Muslim societies there is tendency to equate liberalism with democracy as though these two have the same intellectual source. It is undeniable that liberalism as a political system has been deeply engaged with democratic discourses but it would be a grave mistake to take these two as synonyms. Because there are ample historical as well as intellectual evidences which demonstrate how liberals have resisted democracy as a social movement in the past and there are sufficient reasons to believe that liberalism has distorted democratic ideals by wedding to capitalism and corporatism over against democracy. By democracy, we refer to the consultative role of people in all issues that matter and influence their private and collective life and the transparency at the behest of government in relation to all question that touch upon the life of people in all aspects which fall under the state jurisdiction. Once these issues are taken into consideration then we can realize that current states are not qualified to be considered as democratic either in east or west but Liberal, Socialist, Islamist, Royalist or Despotic systems which attempt to usurp sublime human ideals. Secondly, it will become

clear that democracy is not a western invention but a human creation for improving human societies so they move toward saner
forms of communal life. Thirdly, it should be realized that democracy has been adopted differently by different actors and this
should lead us to understand the complexities which are at work in
politics. In other words, models of governance should be accom-
modated within diverse cultural and historical contexts and no single model could be imposed upon diverse societies across the
globe. Fourthly this should not be also considered as giving license
to submit to despotic models of governance either as we have clearly stated that the consultative principle is an inviolable ideal which
qualify a governmental model to be considered as acceptable or
undesirable. However, it seems there is a tendency among many
scholars in Iran to discern the universal importance of democratic
principle and mistakenly interpret this as an offshoot of modernism,
westernism, liberalism or hedonism. In this chapter, we have come
to argue that the future of many Muslim societies is hinged upon
Islamism but the challenging question before all engaged intellectuals is what kind of Islamism is desirable or even feasible for
tomorrow?

TYPES OF POLITICS

All philosophers, theologians and social theorists since time imme-
morial have tried to define key concepts in their own field of research which they have employed in the body of their respective
theological, sociological or philosophical systems. Allama Jafari is
no exception in this regard. He has reflected upon the concept of
politics and glanced through various existing definitions of politics
and at last has come with his own unique definition. He argues that
"politics in its truest sense means management, justification and
organization of humanity's social life ... on the path of intelligible
life" (Jafari, 2012. 47).

It seems by this definition Allama Jafari has implicitly divided politics into two types, i.e. 1) true politics and 2) artificial politics. In Iran, those thinkers who have refused to work within the parameters of disciplinary rationality tend to ignore not only discursive parameters but also neglect structural dimensions too. For instance, it seems Allama Jafari, by emphasizing on politics in its essential sense, has shied away from actual politics and historical contexts which shape the parameters of political questions. In other words, ignoring political questions in the Iranian context before and after the Iranian Revolution has resulted in an idealistic consecration of certain ideals in early days of Islam during the reign of the Prophet and Imam Ali. I am not critiquing their politics as such, but what is at stake here is that we have not received the existing structures in Muslim societies across the globe thanks to their political models. On the contrary, we are heirs to Umayyad Dynasty, Abbasid Empire, Mongols and many other tribal despotic patterns which have come to shape our historical mentalité as far as politics is concerned. By ignoring these existing structures which have rooted in the hearts and minds of Iranian collectivité we just reproduce them and by idealizing certain ahistorical accounts in the context of politics we are strengthening regressive tendencies in society. In addition, by choosing holy personalities in the Shiite tradition we have consecrated politics in a fashion which does not allow any room for critique or critical engagement as critiquing holy person has come to mean questioning the divine legitimacy. Of course, any critical observer knows that this is not the case but by politicizing the masses a very dangerous dragon has been unleashed within the fabric of society which is impossible to control in a simple fashion. Another issue which I have remarked earlier in Allama Jafari's discourse is the *consecration of politics* that has created a serious problem for the Islamic Republic of Iran. The system has been built upon two pillars theoretically and structurally, i.e. religion and publicity of jurisprudential interpretation of religion by the people. But it seems by consecrating the jurisprudential interpretation of religion the people's significance gets minimized and their votes get less importance. It seems Allama Jafari's reading of politics strengthens this undemocratic position within the Islamic Republic in a fundamental fashion. He argues that "politics [based on the parameters of the intelligible life] ... is the same as the sacred phenomenon ... which ... when it is carried out as it ought to be ... it is one of the most precious human endeavors" (2012. 47).

In the light of this essentialist approach to politics which is deeply widespread among Islamist thinkers and activists across the Muslim World (and even beyond the conventional borders of the House of Islam) one can discern a dominant institutionalized ideology with a particular mentalité within the social collectivité in Iran which is deeply idealistic and anti-historical. If these remarks bear any relevance then my question to Allama Jafari is "if this sacred phenomenon, i.e. politics, has not been carried out in a *right fashion* in a specific political system, in that case what is the duty of people?" To put it differently, how could people stand up against those in power who assumedly are preoccupied with a sacrosanct activity? It seems this point is the Achilles' heel of political thought in Iran (and the entire Muslim World both geographically and intellectually). In other words, Allama Jafari states clearly what ought to be in regard to politics but he marginalizes the historical-sociological dimensions of political structures and the limits of agency in the Iranian context and this perspective is not solely confined to his analysis. On the contrary, it constitutes the very textures of political anthropology in Iran today. In order to understand this culture of politics we need to contextualize it within a larger paradigm of Islamism.

POLITICAL ISLAM

What is the position of political Islam in Allama Jafari's thought? Is there any relation between Allama Jafari's political thought and Islamism? In answering these questions we need to look at his life and work in a synoptic fashion, as considered separately, they may not lead us to an appropriate conclusion. By looking at his biography one may tend to believe that Allama Jafari was not generally interested in politics. While we know that the Islamist discourse has been one of the most challenging political discourses in Iran in the last hundred years nevertheless judging by his activities during two tumultuous decades after the establishment of the Islamic Republic one may assume that Allama Jafari did not get involve in challenges which lay before the system either practically or theoretically. Besides it is undeniable that one of the most celebrated political revolutions in the contemporary era has been a product of the leadership of religious seminaries of Qom and Najaf under the guidance of a Shiite Grand Ayatollah. In other words, the assumed silence of Allama Jafari in this context seems to be very surreal and far from the truth. This question has intrigued me and consequently I approach Allama Jafari's political discourse in a problematical fashion by deconstructing his political ideas without trying to read into his texts either post-reformist or post-conservative ideals which have come to dominate the Iranian political arena since the Green Disobedience Movement in 2009. With these concerns in mind when Allama Jafari's political discourse is approached then it becomes clear that he is in favor of Islamism in an overall fashion but he is actively engaged in *essential refinement* of Islamism. This is to argue that he does not critique actual incidents within the system, nor does he engage in improving institutional departments within the current political system, but instead he refines indirectly the normative system by referring those who are holding governing posts to follow the prophetic or imamatic examples. In order to back up our conclusion on Allama Jafari's conditional agreement with the general paradigm of political Islam we can look at his distinguished work on politics, i.e. *Philosophical Principles of Politics in Islam* where he demonstrates his political manifesto in a very lucid fashion. In this book, Allama Jafari engages on the importance of politics in the parameters of Islam by holding that

> the definition of politics, … its significance, its necessity, and politics … being equal to worship [i.e. being considered as a religious act which ought to be upheld by every single individual in the society] … is similar to what late Ayatollah Seyyed Hasan Modaress … used to state when asked about his position on politics as a religious scholar … that our religiosity is the same as our politics and our politics is the same as our religiosity. (2012. 48)

This is the nub of Political Islam in contemporary Iran and the jurisprudential system based on the doctrine of *authority of the jurist* as it has redefined the principles of republicanism since 1979. In other words, by referring to the Modaressian approach to the mutual relationship between politics and religion Allama Jafari seems to demonstrate its allegiance to Islamism. The differences between Allama Jafari and other Islamist scholars are not of kind but degree. This is to argue that Allama Jafari agrees that the government and state should become religious (i.e. religious state) and follow the jurisprudential prescripts but he is worry about processes which may end up by turning religion into a state property where religion follows governmental guidelines (i.e. governmental religion) under the pretext of Islam. To put it differently, religion should define the boundaries of political activities and structures but there are dangers that we keep the banner of religion but under this pretext apply the Machiavellian principles of power. This is what worried Allama Jafari and the panacea he recommended was to take the ideals of the Prophet and Imams rather than Leviathans.

Here there are issues which we need to discuss as the relations between the state and religion have become one of the key questions in modern social theory and political science and political philosophy. The Russian social thinker and novelist Fyodor Dostoevsky was one of the early proponents of religionizing society on the face of modern challenges which allegedly drove humanity to the brink of annihilation. Reading his works as a critical commentary on deficiencies of modernity one could realize that Dostoevsky arrived at a novel conclusion on the nature of modern society and its impacts on human existence as an image of God. He argued that two institutions of state and religion have grown too separate from each other and the state under the impact of modern principles has transformed the true spirit of religion by emptying it from its essential ideals. He considered this process as creation of a new form of religiosity which is of governmental or state-dependent nature. To counter this, Dostoevsky believed that the state should be transformed into a religious state where religion and the principles inferred from religious canon ought to reign supreme. There are similarities between these issues and what disciplinary sociologists and academic social theorists in the 20th century have conceptualized as secularization thesis or theory but there are also differences which are not directly relevant to this debate here at hand. However, the Iranian revolution of 1979 seems to have similarities to Dostoevsky's discourse on state and religion where modern societies cannot escape from the grand apparatus of state as an all-inclusive institution but this all-inclusive leviathan should be tamed and domesticated in line with religious principles. Allama Jafari seems to follow this overall approach in his political philosophy where he refers to Ayatollah Modaress as his political model (Abrahamian, 1982).

EUROCENTRISM AND POLITICS IN A
CRITICAL BALANCE

Allama Jafari inquires in his *Philosophical Principles of Politics in Islam* into history of political ideas based on a non-Eurocentric perspective. He believes that academics and scholars globally have come under the spell of an *Eurocentric* vision of life, in general, and history of politics, in particular. He holds that

> in recent time ... either we look at eastern academic circles or western scholarly circles ... one can discern a very peculiar tendency among scholars... who work on scientific or philo- sophical issues ... and that is ... whenever they start working on a problem ... they pay homage to Greece by finding the roots of any specific problem there ... as though everything started in Greece .... Nobody can deny the significance of Greece in the history of sciences and philosophical systems ... but this fact should not drive us to an extreme position whereby ... overlook- ing the importance of philosophers, thinkers and authors who belong to other cultures and societies. (2012. 50-1)

This critique is of great significance for those who are not inter- ested in conceptualizing social sciences solely on Eurocentric bases. Let me give you an example on how Allama Jafari was working within the parameters of a non-Eurocentric social science without refusing to employ the best research done by academic scholars and researchers who happened to work within the parame- ters of Eurocentric episteme. Within social theory there has been a longstanding debate on *labor theory of value* and those who are engaged on this question tend to think that this problem has been conceptualized firstly by classical economists in England and then in its critical fashion by Karl Marx in Germany. Allama Jafari does recognize the importance of labor's value in human society but when he attempts to conceptualize this issue he does not look at Europe. On the contrary, in a creative fashion, he argues that "it is well-known that ... the labor theory of value ... has been discussed by social thinkers ... since Ibn Khaldun to the present time" (Jafari, 2013. 295-6).

This reference by Allama Jafari may seem a very simple gesture but this should be considered as a very creative *research program* due to the fact that he critiqued the widespread Eurocentrism which was practiced by scholars around the world and also he attempted to demonstrate how a non-Eurocentric approach could be theoretically, methodologically and practically realized in a scientific paradigm. Of course, Allama Jafari did not employ the concept of Eurocentrism when critiquing contemporary Eurocentric tendencies among scholars globally but there are many indications in his work that clearly demonstrates what Syed Farid Alatas in *Alternative Discourses in Asian Social Science: Responses to Eurocentrism* has masterfully depicted as the pitfalls of Eurocentric approaches in social sciences.

ABSENCE OF POLITICS IN THE EMPIRE OF ISLAM

One may wonder whether prior to modernity and Iran's encounter with the West there was no trace of an independent field of inquiry which took care of political questions. In other words, is it feasible to assume that politics as a branch of knowledge did not exist in Iran and the World of Islam? Allama Jafari is himself concerned about this question and conceptualizes this problem in a critical fashion by arguing that "it is inconceivable ... that a civilization could successfully emerge and grow rapidly on the global stage ... without having a reasonable political system and functioning administrative order" (2012. 58). It is worthy to note that Allama Jafari is aware that

> in the early days ... or even first centuries of Islam ... we cannot see certain codified laws or independent principles ... apart from other general aspects of governing human society ...

erected autonomously in the Empire of Islam ... under the banner of political laws, principles or regulations of Islam .... In other words, political principles of Islam were embedded implicitly ... which have not been articulated yet. (Jafari, 2012. 58)

Allama Jafari believes that the absence of an autonomous discourse on politics is not related to *Iranian political structures* or even *coercive governing bodies* in the World of Islam. In other words, his approach is more of an *epistemological* nature rather than *political sociology* which looks at structures, agency, relations between state and society, class, race, gender, ethnicity, religion, denomination, family structures, bureaucracy, and many other sociopolitical factors which have shaped the body-politics in the course of history in a specific cultural context. Allama Jafari states explicitly that the factors which have contributed to the lack of establishment of politics as an autonomous field of inquiry are not political but epistemological. He believes that the absence of politics as an independent field of inquiry has a very

serious reason ... that experts in schools of Islam are acquainted with ... and that crucial reason is ... unity of all aspects of human existence such as economic, political, legal, moral, artistic and all possible human dimensions. (Jafari, 2012. 58-9)

Allama Jafari touches upon one of the most critical problems which has inflicted modern mentalité and that is the question of compartmentalization of knowledge. In his view, the geometry of human cognition consists of an indivisible unity which, if it is troubled, could create serious problems for humanity at large (2013. 342). This is a very interesting point which Allama Jafari refers to, but the question still remains intact and that is the absence of politics as a field of inquiry within the Empire of Islam, in general, and Iran, in particular. In other words, the epistemological inquiries of Allama Jafari in regard to politics are, in fact, worth to be taken into consideration but the question is whether his etiology is accurate or this *epistemic contraction* in the field of political thought is itself one of the structural problems in the Muslim World Order which was under *tribal mentalities* since the collapse of Sassanid World Order. This is a point which is worth to be studied and Allama Jafari seems to be totally oblivious about its significance in his political reflections.

DESIGNING OF SOCIAL LIFE

Allama Jafari assigns a good deal of discussion in his *Philosophical Principles of Politics in Islam* to the question of societal management, i.e. how to engineer, organize, manage, or govern society. The term he employs in conceptualizing this problem is of great significance, i.e. *Tanzim*. This word has an Arabic root which comes from the term *Nazm*, i.e. "order" in English language. The opposite of *Nazm* or order is *Fesad* or Disorder/Chaos. It seems Allama Jafari is working with these binary oppositions in his political analyses too. Why do I assume this? In the aforementioned work, which could be considered as the political manifesto of Allama Jafari, there are ample references which could be used in strengthening this conclusion. On *Designing or Ordering the Social Life* (2012. 59) Allama Jafari states that

> lack of intervention in ordering of social life ... would be a deviation from the path of Islam ... but political issues and ideas which have been proposed in Islam ... by taking into consideration the amount of such politically-oriented verdicts ... it is sufficient to realize that it is solely ... Islam which could take care of ordering and management of humanity's intelligible life in society. (Jafari, 2012. 59)

In this passage it is clear that Allama Jafari is endorsing the interventionist approach but he is either consciously or unconsciously giving in to state-totalitarianism without mentioning state. On the contrary, he argues that non-interventionist approach would be a deviation from Islam. If one deconstructs the word Islam here it will be straightforwardly apparent that this term does not refer to Islam as a *revealed religion* but a particular reading of Islamic traditions which has come to be known as Islamism or Political Islam in the 20th century. In addition, what Allama Jafari is doing here is making state more powerful by creating a totalitarian state, on the one hand, and marginalizing civil society (and its actor-networks and systems), on the other hand. Moreover, there is another dimension to Allama Jafari's approach which has been clearly stated in the aforementioned episode, i.e. Islam's all-comprehensible capacity in managing humanity's life in all fronts. Needless to argue that this is one of the key assumptions of Islamism which Allama Jafari has uncritically accepted and in accordance to this paradigm he has constructed "Islam's Vision" of reality in its broadest sense. In other words, Allama Jafari has taken Islamism or the jurisprudential vision of politics as the only true interpretation of revelation and based on this reading he has constructed the good life. To put it differently, he argues that by ordering the parameters of intelligible life in society we are able to lead the social order toward "intelligible freedom" (Jafari, 2012. 59).

INTELLIGIBLE FREEDOM

When the approach towards politics is of theological nature then the frame of reference would be surely textual or text-centered. Another approach could be of sociological nature which would transform the contours of analysis by focusing more on historical dimensions which have given birth to socio-cultural and political structures that are reflected in the textures of agency too. Of course, this does not mean that these approaches could not be combined as a whole but there are shortcomings which could lead to a blind idealism as it has been the case with Islamist discourses which cannot distinguish between text and con-text. For instance, Allama

Jafari touches upon the question of political freedom without making any reference to structural dimensions, institutional aspects, or any contextual limits which may exist in realizing freedom in the political sense of the term within the parameters of a nation-state. He argues that there are many canonical verdicts and sacred verses

> which refer abundantly to ... the removal of obstacles ... barriers ... and troublesome ... as well as oppressive ... bondages ... which taken as a harmonic whole would create the necessary context for the erection of intelligible life ... which ... would, in turn, result in the emergence of intelligible freedom. Certainly all these verses and verdicts are sufficient to prove the pivotal significance of political dimension in the constitution of human life in Islam. (2012. 59)

These are interesting remarks but it is not clear that Allama Jafari is referring to the Iranian political context or other contemporary political systems which lack what he considers to be "intelligible freedom." In other words, if these are to be considered as critiques leveled at liberal, social-democratic, socialist, or even conservative political systems or societies then one needs to ask whether one could have intelligible freedom in political sense without having democratic institutions which would allow unconstrained (free from oppressions) communication in the public square. On the other hand, if Allama Jafari is talking about other systems or contexts then one is left with a big question-mark as there are no concrete references to any historical case or social system. If one argues that these discussions are of philosophical order in regard to politics then one is left amazed why Allama Jafari is critiquing contemporary western societies without comparing them with political structures or political culture of contemporary Iran. On the contrary, he compares western political contexts and structures with Islamic texts. This is a fallacious syllogism or misleading comparative approach which has inflicted many Islamist scholars and theorists since the early days of 20th century. Of course, this is not to deny that Allama Jafari in his *Philosophical Principles of Politics in Islam* has paid scant attention to historical dimensions which may have influenced the state of politics as a field of inquiry by conceptualizing politics as an intellectual imagination which has been under the tutelage of Sunnite interpretation of the revealed tradition. This is a view which needs to be appraised in details critically.

Chapter Five

Revisiting the Principle of
Divine Authority

INTRODUCTION

One of the challenging questions before scholars and intellectuals who attempt to engage social and political issues is one's loyalty or disloyalty toward "historical context." In other words, what are the dangers of addressing sociopolitical issues in an ahistorical fashion? Many contemporary Iranian political jurists seem to approach politics in an ahistorical manner and the outcomes of these kinds of anachronistic approaches could be considered unsuccessful if they are taken to be as policy or policy-making manuals for running nation-state systems. In this chapter, we have revisited the principle of divine authority in Allama Jafari's frame of reference and argued that if this approach is not critically appraised then we shall get stuck in perennial dilemmas as juristic arguments should not be treated in an atemporal fashion as social governance need to be anchored in the soil of democracy, i.e. consultation, public debate, equality and de-sanctification of power.

POLITICS AND THE SUNNITE INTERPRETATION

Since the establishment of Islamism as a form of governance in
Iran there have been many different approaches to politics and
society in the context of Iranian culture which is argued to be
allegedly intertwined with religion in a profound fashion. Intellectuals have contested each other by arguing that religion is the
source of all ills in Iran, on the one hand, and other intellectuals
have gone to the other extreme by arguing that the panacea of all
ills in Iran (and even the world) is to return to religion as a model of
organizing society and as a mold of categorizing the human mind.
Some have gone so extreme such as Aramesh Doostar by arguing
that in Iran there has never been any trace of critical thinking or
thinking in its sociological sense rather than theological sense
which is deeply concerned with human eschatology. Again we can
see the works of other Iranian thinkers such as Seyed Javad Tabata-
bai who believes that the Iranian political thought is in its declining
phase. There are yet others who argue that we are in a state of
refusal, i.e. the Iranian mentalité has become so obsessed with theological concepts that it is not capable of engaging on pressing
sociopolitical questions in the context of *polis*. Of course, it is
needless to argue that religious intellectuals after 1979 have tried to
counter these critiques but the inner logic of authoritarian interpretation of Islamism has eschewed them from the public sphere *in
toto*. In other words, religious intellectualism as an intellectual
stream with political significance has been pushed away from me-
dia, academia, seminaries and all important sites of authority. At
any rate, between opposite poles of refusal and possibility of thinking about communal life of individuals which is the subject-matter
of politics, we can carve out a position for Allama Jafari who seems
to deny the importance of the refusal-paradigm, but at the same
time attempts to go beyond the *paradigm of eventuality*. Of course,
it is not clear how Allama Jafari wants to overcome his theological
inclinations as far as politics is concerned but there are certain signs

in his *Philosophical Principles of Politics in Islam* that convinces us to conclude that he is trying to locate politics in a historical context rather than theological text. Under a section which is dedicated to political inquiries within the empire of Islam, Allama Jafari approaches historical events which have been instrumental in shaping the contours of politics in the Muslim context. Of course, it is interesting to note that Allama Jafari does not pay systematic attention to social structures in sociological sense but in this rare occasion it seems that he is embarking upon a novel route in his political inquiries. By constructing a *Sunni Interpretation of Religion* and explaining the decline of political imagination in the World of Islam by reference to the dominant Sunni institutes, one can doubtlessly state that Allama Jafari has gone sociological rather than theological in this context. He states that,

> we are faced with a kind of historical trend ... which should be studied carefully so ... its underlying streams could be unearthed. The real question is that ... issues, principles and rules which are of pivotal significance in political philosophy of Islam ... often have not been either discussed extensively within scientific paradigms or explicated comprehensively within jurisprudential frameworks... or even ... followed by statesmen in practice .... Now we need to ask about the underlying problems which have given rise to this complex political situation. Firstly ... it should be noted that dynasties and governments which ruled the empires in the world of Islam ... followed the Sunnite school formally .... On the other hand, due to the fact that during the most part of history in the vast Muslim regions ... until very recent time ... Muslim societies were run by Sunnite rulers ... which meant Shiite scholars did not have any say in political matters .... This factual state of affairs led to undertheorization of political issues, problems and principles ... by jurists and experts who did not feel any necessity in indulging in politics. (Jafari, 2012. 59)

Here Allama Jafari refers to two important points; the first is the rulers' absence of compliance to Islamic political principles and the second is the lack of Shiite scholars' involvement in politics until the recent period. Although these are very important issues which Allama Jafari has raised, they need to be debated extensively in a critical fashion. Needless to argue that what Allama Jafari considers as the recent period is equivalent to 500 years, i.e. since the establishment of the Safavid Dynasty in 1501. In other words, to blame the lack of political field of inquiry on the Sunni interpretation and the rules of dynasties which complied formally with the Sunni reading of principles of political philosophy of Islam is not a consistent scholarship. Because political problems which were dominant in the Sunni Ottoman Empire such as despotism, suppression, oppressive policies towards the "other," and many other despotic ruling styles occurred similarly in the Shiite Safavid Empire. To put it differently, the dissidence (in politics) and heresy (in religion) were punished severely without any difference either in the Sunni realm of governance or the Shiite realm of governance. Now to ascribe the lack of political thought to the Sunni interpretation would not be sufficient as a scholarly explanation. I think there are more issues which should be discussed but the frame of reference needs to be sociological rather than theological or metaphysical. Besides, the realm of the Safavid dynasty coincided with the emergence of the transcendent philosophy of Mulla Sadra (1571–1640) who was a contemporary of René Descartes (1596–1650) but the question is why the emergence of a Shiite governing body did not have any reflection in Sadra's philosophy and more importantly why he was forced to leave the public sphere in a Shiite political milieu. In other words, why was the philosophical mode of analysis unwelcomed in Iran but the Cartesian mode of philosophical analysis was welcomed in France? The problem is not Sunni or Shiite in denominational sense of these schools. On the contrary, the question is which interpretation is more conducive for free-thinking and dialogical mode of understanding. If we do not take into considerations these sociological parameters we shall get into old traps as the present experiences in Iran demonstrate clearly that if undemocratic assumptions, despotic modes of engagements and totalitarian approaches towards dissidence and heresy are not critically appraised then it does not matter formally if you establish a Shiite political body or a Sunni realm of governance. Allama Jafari seems to be oblivious to these delicate issues which are crucial in any political discourse.

SOVEREIGNTY IN ISLAM

One of the most challenging problems of thinking among Iranian thinkers (and the World of Islam) is that fundamental questions are either conceptualized in reference to occidental categories or in the context of Islam. What is the meaning of this judgment? The West is consisted of a group of distinct countries which have different socio-politico-cultural systems that have emerged in the context of particular experiences of Western Europe with a specific form of Christianity—which is fundamentally unlike the Iranian complex society. Unpardonably in Iran these differences have been neglected by many modern leading scholars who have attempted to impose the European experience of modernity on all aspects and dimensions of the Iranian society. On the other hand, there are many leading scholars and intellectuals who put the West as the opposite of Islam when, for instance, discussing issues related to politics. In other words, as though the "other" of Islam is the West or vice versa which leads to a particular strategy in constructing contemporary mindset among scholars, intellectuals, thinkers and philosophers in Iran. To put it differently, by arguing in this manner, the proponents of this strategy seek to argue that the ideological equal of the West (and its various ideological systems and schools of philosophy) is Islam and the latter is superior to the West due to fundamental deficiencies which have enveloped the West as a form of civilization—which has led to alienation of contemporary humanity. The problem in this comparative strategy which is very dominant today among people in the World of Islam is that Islam is a religion which is not comparable with western political/ideological/economic systems or even with the West (as a variable geographical entity). If one is insisting to compare Islam the equal should have the same quality, i.e. the equal of Islam is another religious system which is not based solely on reason and empirical cognition of reality. In other words, Islam should be compared with other world religions. To compare Islam with socialism, liberalism, communism and conservatism is not only wrong in an ethical sense but fundamentally false in philosophical sense of the term. However this false attitude has become so dominant and penetrated in the deep corners of collective mind that one can speak of a common error (i.e. solecism) which it is impossible to be demonstrated to thinkers who use this false comparative strategy in their research program. There is another important point which we need to take into consideration in this context, i.e. Islam versus the West. Assuming that we can compare these two entities, the problem is that Islam as a *text* cannot be compared with the West as a *context*. In other words, if we attempt to force, at any cost, this comparative strategy on these two incomparable entities, then how could Islam, in its textual form, be compared to contemporary western political systems which have been actualized in contextual forms. To put it differently, the *actual* could not be compared with the *ideal*. Comparison as a form of intellectual engagement has certain logical requirements which cannot arbitrarily be neglected.

After this brief critical assessment of the political context in the World of Islam, I would like to turn to Allama Jafari's approach in this regard. In my reading of Allama Jafari, I have come to realize that he employs the same false comparative strategy by comparing Islam and the West. In other words, he considers the two as equal comparative entities and argues that Islam is superior to the West. There are two issues here which should be tackled. The first issue is that the problem is not the superiority or inferiority of Islam which is at stake. On the contrary, this false *othering strategy* deprives us from having an empirical picture of actual state of affairs. If one looks at the entire political discourse of Allama Jafari it will be clear that he is deeply oblivious towards the actual state of politics and political structures in Iran (and the World of Islam). By following this entrenched *othering strategy* Allama Jafari does not study, critique and analyze the actual institutions, forms, patterns, processes and projects of power in Iran. In other words, what should be, as a matter of fact, compared are sociopolitical systems in the World of Islam (Iran) and Western or European systems and political orders. Because it is this second kind of comparative scheme which could open up the ways for improvements of actual state of affairs without falling in the cognitive trap of comparing two incomparable entities of Islam and the West. The second issue which Allama Jafari does not show any sensitivity about is the very concept of "Islam." By laying claim on "Islam," Allama Jafari is inadvertently arguing that his reading of the tradition is the only true interpretation of the revealed religion. It is clear that the "Islam" in this context does not refer to the revealed tradition but to a particular reading of Islamic traditions which is known as *Islamism* or *Political Islam*. These assumptions have not been articulated by Allama Jafari or anyone who adheres to the jurisprudential interpretation of the revealed tradition in Iran. These are disputable assumptions which we need to challenge but to challenge them in Iran today it is not very easy as religion has become deeply politicized and politics has become profoundly jurisprudentialized in the public square and the Iranian imagined society.

Now after this lengthy introduction we should get back to the question of "sovereignty" which has been conceptualized by Allama Jafari within the parameters of what he terms as Islam but it should be interpreted as Islamism or the paradigm of Political Islam. He argues that

> the principle of divine sovereignty ... [is a fundamental proposition] ... in political philosophy of Islam ... which is agreed upon by the majority of experts who are well-versed in the philosophy of the Islamic tradition. Needless to argue that this proposition is different from theocracy which was dominant in Europe during the Middle Ages ... which was based on depriving people from having any participatory role in determining their own sociopolitical destiny. (2012. 393)

If the political principle of the *divine sovereignty* in Islam is different than theocracy and neglecting people's right in politics is wrong and alien to the jurisprudential model of governance then what kind of role do people play in a non-theocratic political system which is based on the principle of the divine sovereignty? Is the role of people formal or substantial in the constitution of the political system designed by Islamism? In other words, the people do not play any substantial role in regard to *legitimacy* of the system but their role is important in terms of *acceptance* of the political order. The distinction between legitimacy and acceptance is a novel jurisprudential conceptualization which has become current in the post-Revolutionary Iranian Islamist political discourses which assume that these two are distinct issues in kind but interrelated for the sake of social cohesion. Within the Islamist jurisprudential paradigm the legitimacy of the political order is assessed by the level of system's compliance to *Sharia* and hence it's *Mashruiya* (i.e. legitimacy in accordance to theological principles which have been explicated in the sacred canons). This legitimacy is different than the Rousseauian or Hobbesian definition of legitimacy which is defined within sociopolitical parameters of a given society. However, if we accept the distinction between legitimacy and acceptance as it has been conceptualized within the Islamist frame of jurisprudence then a question may arise in terms of the nature and place of people's recognition separate from legitimacy. In other words, one should ask whether people's acceptance is of essential significance for the constitution of an Islamist political order or its importance is only formal or decorative. In order to be able to assess these questions we need to have an empirical approach to politics and its institutions in Iran and the World of Islam as without such an approach we cannot fathom the state of politics in these aforementioned contexts. To put it differently, by ascribing the declining state of political thought to the dominant Sunni interpretation of Islam would not resolve the problems of political sovereignty in Shiite discourses on politics. In addition to these reflections we need to question the widespread attitude towards political thought in the Shiite context which aims to conceptualize Shiite discourses in their ideal forms without taking into consideration cycles of historical political developments which have transformed the contours of politics in the Shiite context. For instance, what is Allama Jafari's stance toward the *Constitutional Movement* which took place in the heart of the Shiite World based on his principle of divine sovereignty? Allama Jafari approaches the question of political sovereignty through Imam Ali's letter to Malek Ashtar which took place in 7th century where the latter was supposed to hold office in Egypt. Allama Jafari does not make clear how politics should be conceptualized in Iran which has been transformed through constitutionalism at the hands of Grand Ayatollahs such as Akhund Khorasani and Mirza Reza Naini, on the one hand, and Ayatollah Sheikh Fazlollah Nuri, on the other hand. The battles between constitutionalists and canonicalists (i.e. those who endorsed the rule of Shah without any restrictions and then moved toward another position by proposing the rule of Sharia and finally arrived at the rule of Jurist) left serious scars on the body of Iranian politics since 1907 which finally caused the second Iranian Revolution in 1979 under the leadership of Ayatollah Khomeini who opposed the despotism and anti-Constitutional rule of Shah since the

1953 *Iranian coup d'état.* These significant historical developments within the context of Shiite politics had no resonance within the entire gamut of Allama Jafari's political thought. This is what I call blind idealism which has struck different trends among Islamism where actual issues are neglected for various reasons but instead ideal forms of politics are discussed in details without any relation to existing political structures which affect the actual patterns of agency in Iran (and the World of Islam). There are few examples in the Iranian context which one could mention in passing, i.e. Ayatollah Seyyed Mahmud Taleghani who had a more egalitarian-Islamist approach towards power, on the one hand, and engaged critically with the existing totalitarian political structures which restricted freedom and liberty of subjects, on the other hand.

Allama Jafari spend the last twenty years of his active intellectual life during the Islamist political system (i.e. 1979–1999) which was ruled under the authority of jurisprudential model of governance where purportedly the state claimed to implement religious ideals as interpreted within the Shiite tradition by pious scholars. In his *Philosophical Principles of Politics in Islam* Allama Jafari distinguishes categorically between Christian model of theocracy and Islam's model of divine governance by arguing that in the former there is no room for people's participatory role while in the latter people have a significant function in the running of the affairs (2012. 393). Granted this distinction is feasible but the problem has not been solved yet as sociological evidences contradict Allama Jafari's theological position on the dissimilarity between the principle of divine authority in Islam and the principle of theocracy in Christianity. Why do I argue in this fashion? My Sociological observations lead me to think that what Allama Jafari conceptualizes as Islam's principle of politics is Islamist interpretation of the revealed tradition of Islam and these two are deeply distinguished and one should not assume that the twain are identical. Because in doing so we turn Islam into an ideological paradigm which is reduced to Islamism similar to Liberalism, Communism, Socialism, Conservatism, Marxism and other dominant political ideologies of modern era. In addition, this reductionist act of turning Islam into Islamism closes the doors of novel interpretation (i.e. *Ijtihad* which is an intellectual Jihad) within the World of Islam under the pretext of national security or disintegration of the political system and so on and so forth. Moreover it is not certain that the Islamist interpretation of the divine authority will be in practice any different than the oppressive theocratic model of governance which was implemented during the Middle Ages in the Christian World. In other words, one could ask Allama Jafari whether the dominant trend in the context of Islamic Republic of Iran has not been in favor of transforming the divine authority into a theocratic model of governance as we had in Europe. Because if Allama Jafari would argue against this claim then one needs to look at the sociological context which provide us with abundant evidence in this regard but his approach is backed up again by a theological reading of the text without taking into consideration sociopolitical facts, realities and context. The present political realities in Iran seem to point toward a theocratic interpretation of Islamism which is even more totalitarian than the old Christian model which Europe experienced due to historical complexities of modern state machineries that were absent during the Middle Ages. I think this theocratic trend is becoming more visible and louder within the context of Iranian politics due to various reasons which should be taken into consideration if we are serious about removal of obstacles toward a more egalitarian model of governance in Iran and the World of Islam. One of these problems is the negligence of the context which has led to elevation of text to an inaccessible position in the Islamist political discourses in Iran where political actors shy away from sociological analyses which have led to contemporary deadlock and instead critique the present policies by reference to textual prophetic and imamatic models in the early days of Islam. In other words, the lack of attention to particular political, social, cultural and intellectual structures and patterns in Allama Jafari's political paradigm does only aggravate the obstruction of creative political thinking in Iran. We need to take into consideration actual political structures more seriously as they constitute and determine the boundaries of social actions and outmost possibilities of political agency in Iran today. Without realizing these limits and possibilities we cannot envision the nature of actual constrictions which have been pulling down the progressive attempts of Iranians since the Constitutional Revolution in 1907 and the Islamist Revolution of 1979. In my view, what is need to be done urgently in the context of Iranian political thought is to move the dominant theological approach toward a more sociological perspective within the context of politics so one could be able to distinguish between the *ideal* and the *actual* as they are presently mixed up in a critical fashion. In other words, the brief experiences of Prophet Mohammad's and Imam Ali's political governance did not shape the collective contours of Muslim mentalité and political structures in the World of Islam. On the contrary, we are heirs of political attitudes and visions of various kingdoms such as Umayyad, Abbasid, Mongols and Pahlavi dynasties respectively. Unless one pays attention to analyses of "historical contexts" more one tends toward utopianism and turns also inattentive before sociopolitical realities which result in sacralizing existing despotic structures that are present in every corner of the Iranian sociopolitical context.

REVISITING THE PRINCIPLE OF DIVINE AUTHORITY

Within the Shiite political thought there is a tendency toward appointment rather than election. In other words, Shiite scholars argue that the governing of Medina or Polis is not a matter of consensus but divine appointment. This is to argue that authority needs to be founded upon a legitimate ground but this legitimacy within the Shiite political thought is not achieved through consensus or people within a particular political entity. On the contrary, it is argued that the right to govern is endowed upon by God and the process of endowment of power is of divine order. To put it differently, authority as a right is determined by God but this should not be associated with imposition of authority and sovereignty right. The Shiite scholars have tried to argue against critics who have charged the Shiite scholars of being proponents of autocratic rule or dictatorship by distinguishing between appointment and imposition. The dominant argument by grand Shiite scholars could be reconstructed as permission in terms of divine appointment but prohibition in regard to imposition of authority. In other words, if one interprets the divine appointment within the Shiite political tradition as permission in imposing the appointed governor without people's consent then this is against the idea of divine authority or a breach, in the parlance of jurists, of purpose (which is leading humanity towards higher ideals of being). However the challenging question is not only the ideals within political thought of Shiism but historical structuration of these grand ideals which have shaped collective patterns of actions, mentalité and institutions in Iran and the World of Islam. In other words, how and under what circumstances could people check and balance the appointed governing body or ruler in the context of contemporary globalized nation-state? To put it differently, if for some reasons people have accepted the appointed-by-proxy ruler but under different circumstances, or due to the bad policies designed by the ruler or the government, people may opt for change, then what are the actual mechanisms for realizing their political demands? This is to argue, what are the political criteria for distinguishing or measuring between "imposition" and "appointment"? Is the textual reference the arbiter in political conflicts or patterns of political actions and decision-making policies the basis for political judgment? By reading dominant historical discourses on politics among Shiite and Sunni scholars one can readily conclude that textual imagination takes precedence over contextual understanding and this trend has become aggravated within the Islamist discourses today, in general, and in Iran, in particular. Allama Jafari as a prime example of this textual trend within political schools of Islamism; he demonstrates prominent aspects of this intellectual malaise which has inflicted the body of politics in the World of Islam. By proposing the principle of divine authority, Allama Jafari attempts to reconstruct this principle in relation to *national consent* which is a modern principle that was not seriously conceptualized in political schools in the East and the World of Islam. He does not even concede that consent as a political tool is an egalitarian concept which has become institutionalized within modern context of politics and by neglecting this significant achievement he downplays the significant role of modern institutional structures which are capable of checking and balancing power institutions. Allama Jafari argues that by accepting the principle of divine authority we could arrive at a very important conclusion and that is

> the acceptance of divine principle of authority is of extraordinary significance due to the fact that ... the faith of ... the ruler and ... people who live under its governorship which is based on their belief to Allah ... and Allah's all-comprehensible supervision over the entire gamut of reality ... and even their own existence ... and the fact that Allah has clearly intended to guide them toward ... the perfect path of intelligible life ... these facts, in other words, would encourage both the ruler and the ruled ... to comply with the intelligible principles of the sacred ... and in a harmonic fashion step forward ... in realizing them. Because by accepting the divine principle of authority ... everybody ... would attempt to ... realize these rules and principles ... without any need ... for resorting to force ... or other involuntary factors .... To put it differently, the acceptance of this divine principle could, at least, prepare the fulfilling atmosphere ... in a given society so people could ... prepare themselves ... in aspiring towards the divine ideals .... (2012. 393-4)

Before engaging with this passage I need to mention a very important point in regard to Allama Jafari's concepts in regard to politics. Like many other Shiite scholars he employs mystic concepts which are hard to define or defend in the field of political inquiry. For instance, he uses terms such as "attraction," "perfection," "divine guardianship," and "eagerness" within political debates which are imprecise and elusive on social level. Of course, they may be of crucial importance in poetical frame of mystic contemplations but they create various kinds of confusions when applied in political frame sociological analyses. Apart from this problem, what Allama Jafari argues in this context is not unproblematic either as one needs to ask him if the ruler's faith was not as he claimed then what should people do for throwing away the ruler's unjust authority? In other words, Allama Jafari assumes that faith is what connects the ruler and the ruled before God by creating a divine synergy thanks to the principle of sacred authority which enlightens everyone to seek a life within the parameters of intelligibility regardless of what position one occupies in society, i.e. ruler or ruled. Granted this is a very beautiful ideal but the question remains unanswered, not only by Allama Jafari but the entire Islamist scholars who do not take egalitarian critiques seriously and the question is: what is the duty of people in the absence of a just ruler or oppressive government? Allama Jafari does not address this question for various reasons but this lack of engagement is not confined to him alone as the majority of Islamist scholars within the Islamic Republic of Iran or other Muslim kingdoms or republics shy away from intellectual engagement due to political dangers or inherent intellectual constraints. Although the political dangers are serious, I do not think this is the only reason for dominant intellectual disengagement on behalf of Shiite and Sunnite scholars. On the contrary, I tend to believe that the real issue is of intellectual order and the other problems occupy second or third seats. However, the outcome of this intellectual disengagement is catastrophic as far as political thought is concerned. Because, Allama Jafari and those who follow this pattern of inquiry tend to idealize authority which leads to sacralization of political system (and its leadership) and in doing so they close all possible routes for demonstration of "political opposition" or, at least, not assigning any room for opposition within the system. Needless to argue that within progressive and developed political systems where people are considered as mature citizens and not as immature subjects or what is briefly defined as democratic political order, it could be discerned that the system is consisted of two pillars, i.e. participation and opposition. In other words, the crucial problem within politics and various competing political orders is not "participation" but how to safeguard the rights and security of the opposition or opposing views as this is the criteria for considering a system as good/legitimate or bad/illegitimate. Allama Jafari, on the contrary, approaches political thought in an ahistorical fashion (i.e. without paying attention to historical/political structures within any given context) which leads to a counterproductive mode of political paradigm. To put it differently, it seems Allama Jafari confirms in his own particular way the established jurisprudential dogma that *the authority of jurist is the continuation of prophetic authority*. This indisputable doctrine has given the Islamists within the Iranian post-Revolutionary context the upper hand and a justifiable political tool to excoriate dissidents and anybody who aspires to have a more egalitarian interpretation of Islamism. Of course, Allama Jafari employs a different terminology for expressing the same jurisprudentially-loaded political ideas. For instance, when he talks about *jurisprudential authority* he replaces it by *management office* (2013. 280).

Epilogue

Some time ago, a postmodern savant argued that all that is left is only *image*. There are people who think through concepts and there are people who are more susceptible to images. Conceptually-oriented minds are insensitive to images. They see them but do not perceive them as they should. The *Empire of Google* targets image-oriented people who have grown rapidly in numbers thanks to consolidation of digitalized being in the googlized era. Images speak very loudly and in different contrasting languages simultaneously without realizing their imprints upon the deepest corners of our being which has been reduced into a digitalized being today. By the digitalized being I refer to a dimension of human reality which is in-formed through floods of image-generating data without being thought through or reflected upon due to their colossal quantities. In other words, the digitalized personality is a fragmentized reality that entertains itself in quantitative fashions. "News without views" constitutes the backbones of the digitalized being which is dominated by images today. The Empire of Google is one of the most celebrated emblems of this digitalized era which does not know any imaginary boundaries but it is bounded by boundaries of image. By going through *google.com* one can realize that this demiurge generates all kinds of images and the images which are created by this semi-god could prove decisive in adjudicating the fate of any question that one may have in mind. Islamism as a concept is as old as postmodernity but the image which is generated on the Empire of Google is as negative as one could ever imagine. On the net one does not log in with one's whole being but through her/his digitalized being which is unconsciously ruled by images which pop up before us. One does not read the images on the *net.com* but glances through them and stores them somewhere inactively which would surely influence our judgments actively. Islamism as a modern political ideology has become digitalized and thus *googlized* as a postmodern phenomenon. By post-modernization of Islamism I refer to digital exposure of images of Islamism which have been displayed on the internet in a massive scale that targets virtual landschaft of surfers. In other words, the virtual image of Islamism is negative due to the fact that whatever is related conceptually to Islam has come to be associated with *terror* and hence terrorism. Because the world which we live in is a securitized reality that has stretched its images into the virtual zone too. Although it could be argued that the *net.com* is a neutral arena but it is undeniable that asymmetrical rules of power-games are enforced in googlized context as it is elsewhere. Thus it is not farfetched to imagine that depiction of Islam, Islamism and Terrorism as synonymous images are related to power relations which have found their abodes in the googlized reality as they have already been in place in virtualized dimensions of social life before *googlization of everyday life*. It is argued that Google's mission is to organize the world's information but this is the explicit mission of the Google. The implicit mission of the Google is to form/in-form/re-form the tapestry of human imagination so we, as human agents, take the Google as our common imagined frame of reference. If this is established then if you ask someone why you think that Islam or Islamism is equivalent to Terrorism then the answer would be: *It is on Google!* The Google does not work solely on the conceptual level but it functions on deeper level of human psyche which is of imaginative nature rather than cognitive quality. Once you have seen it then you have pictured it in your mind and when the mental processes have depicted something within your unconscious dimensions of being then you are possessed by images which hunt your digitalized personality. In the googlized world there is not much room for ideas or thoughts in the pre-digitalized sense of these sublime terms due to the fact that we are all connected to the *net* in an obsessive fashion which disables us to think about things we see in a reasonable manner. It should be realized that

> Googlization affects three large areas of human concern and conduct: "us" (through Google's effects on our personal information, habits, opinions, and judgments); "the world" (through the globalization of a strange kind of surveillance and ... infrastructural imperialism); and "knowledge" (through its effects on the use of the great bodies of knowledge accumulated in books, online databases, and the Web). (Vaidhyanathan, 2011. 141)

In this work I did not intend to dwell very much on the Empire of Google as such but I started to focus on images that I came across through googling. By googling I realized that Islamism is portrayed in a very negative fashion but it is easy to conclude that these images are available for millions of viewers on the internet. Once we realize that googlization of life is a social fact as inflation is a social fact today then we become conscious that things need to be re-imagined in different ways. The problem I attempted to tackle is the question of political ideas in Iran (and the Muslim World) through looking at Allama Jafari's political thought as a brilliant example of such a trend. I have mentioned (Miri, 2010, 2012, 2013) elsewhere that Allama Jafari is one of the most creative social thinkers of Iran which is still unknown on the global scale. Here I chose his political thought in relation to one of the most powerful ideological streams in the world today, i.e. Islamism. I attempted to demonstrate through his ideas the relevance of Islamism and the pitfalls of jurisprudentialist dimensions of political Islam which could be overcome if Islamist scholars and thinkers realize that the frame that could accommodate Islamism in a more effective manner is not jurisprudentialist interpretation but democratic frame of reference. I wanted to argue that the Muslim world is not moving toward a post-Islamist era due to the fact that people in Muslim societies tend to have a *visible religiosity* rather than invisible religiosity which is emblematic of Euro-Atlantic societies where the public is more inclined toward an *invisible religiosity*. Here I need to expand on this distinction as this is a theory which I have thought about it for the past three decades thanks to my life in Iran, Turkey, Egypt, Malaysia and Azerbaijan (as Muslim countries), Sweden, Denmark, England and Germany (as Western European countries), Hungary and Bulgaria (as Eastern European countries), Greek (as a Mediterranean country), Ukraine, Belorussia and Russia (as non-European and non-Muslim countries), China, Mongolia and Taiwan (as non-European/non-Christian and non-Muslim but Asian countries) and America (as a new modern global example). In other words, by living in these diverse contexts I have come to realize that we can explain contrasts and commonalities in terms of visible versus invisible religiosity as sociological concepts. However it may be confusing for the readers why I have played with the idea of *Islamism and the Empire of Google* for a work where political ideas of an Iranian social philosopher are at the stake. I can explain this due to the fact that when I wanted to write the first chapter which is an attempt to redraw the contemporary political thought in an Islamist era I came to realize that how images are important in determining our perspectives in a digitalized world where everything has become googlized. My point of departure has been through googlized images which I received through the internet and then realized that how difficult is to dissociate googlized reality from reality of ideas which have been associated with Islamism (as a modern progressive ideology). Of course, it is very hard to speak of terms, concepts, words, notions, ideas and ideals which are in one way or the other related to Islam in a world that has been raped by Neo-conservative corporate artilleries in all fields of *us, the world* and *knowledge*—which have made Islam identical to Terrorism. The military war on terror has its equivalent in the Empire of Google which is skillfully reflected through images which imposes panoptical surveillance on the interior tapestry of human imagination in an unprecedented fashion. This study started with images of Islamism and turned to ideas of Islamism (as a political ideology) in the thought of Allama Jafari and finally come to its end with an argument that the age of Islamism has just begun but more democratic interpretations of Islamism (not Islam) may bring peaceful transformations to the Muslim World and even the geopolitics of tomorrow.

In other words, by looking at one of the significant social theorists in contemporary era I intended to demonstrate that it is a grave mistake to assume the challenges before *Restern Countries* as conflicts between religion and modernity. As far as the Muslim World is concerned the conflict is between competing ideologies which aspire to monopolize the public sphere in autocratic fashions. In other words, the conflict is not between Modernity and Islam and any dichotomization of this kind is doomed to failure due to the fact that religion is not either an ideology or solely a cognitive paradigm. Religion may beget ideology or schools of thought but it is not either an ideology or a school of thought. It is, so to speak, better understood in a Jungian fashion rather than in a Freudian manner which approaches religion in a solely cognitive fashion and therefore finds it as an illusion which shall not have a future in the constitution of a rational self and a rationalized society. In other words, if we assume that there is a conflict then the conflict is between ideologies such as Liberalism and Islamism. In my understanding, within many Muslim countries there is a public demand which could be conceptualized as "Visible Religiosity." This is to argue that the majority in the Muslim countries favors a more visible presence of religion in their public life and this fact is sociologically discernible and hard to deny. This is my first hypothesis. My second hypothesis is that the conflicts which social theorists, sociologists, political scientists and even orientalists (within departments of Middle Eastern Studies) have conceptualized (on religion and modernity) are not, in fact, between Islam and Modernity or Islam and Democracy as these two are not comparable. On the contrary, if there is any conflict or contrast then that is between Islamism and Modernism or Islamism and Democratism. However, it should be mentioned that it seems the real conflict is not between Islamism and Modernism as the former is an offshoot of modernism and the real challenge is whether Islamism is essentially in opposition to Democratism. There are many scholars who would like to take Liberalism as the best frame of democratic reference which has surpassed historical pitfalls of modern ideologies such as Communism, Socialism, Fascism, and Nazism. In other words, the best model which one could fathom democracy is the one provided by Liberalism that has been institutionalized in countries such as America. In addition, there are many scholars who argue that modernity is a path that all successful nations should pass through and the roadmap is the one provided by Euro-Atlantic countries such as France, Germany, England and America. Both of these views are Eurocentric and have been critiqued by many non-Eurocentric intellectuals and thinkers who have argued that democracy is not equivalent to liberalism and it is wrong to assume that the road to modernity could not be fathomed in multiplicities. In other words, one could assume that Islamism is a modern form of reconstructing Muslim societies which differ from the Euro-Atlantic models of social engineering but it would be a remiss to assume that democracy is a western product and inapplicable to Restern societies. My sociological observations lead me to believe that Islamism is the future of the Muslim world in a political sense but at the same time my observations demonstrate that if we don't distinguish between local and universal then the future of Muslim societies would be very gloomy. To put it differently, Islamism needs to be relocated within the parameters of democratic boundaries and one should distance Islamism from regressive and anti-democratic readings which justify their regressive principles on unjustifiable grounds such as incompatibility of Islam and Democracy or incongruity of Islam and Liberalism and clash of Islam and Modernism. As I have argued earlier, in the modern context which Muslim societies find themselves the comparisons are not between Islam and aforementioned ideologies. On the contrary, the real comparison is between Islamism which is the dominant ideology in these countries where we can witness other ideologies such as communism, nationalism, liberalism and socialism. But the dominant trend which has shaped the public sphere in a fundamental fashion is the ideology of Islamism. This ideology, due to various socio-cultural factors, has leaned more toward despotism, autocratic rule and jurisprudentialism rather than democratic interpretations of social governmentality and politics. We should realize that Liberalism is a Eurocentric vision of governing society which could be of great importance in many western societies but it will not work properly in countries such as Iran where "Visible Religiosity" is favored in the public sphere. Of course, this does not mean that Iran is a more religious country than America or Sweden where the public sphere is better understood in terms of "Invisible Religiosity." This could only mean that different societies express distinctly their symbolic realities both on individual levels and social dimensions. There is no reference to normative superiority or inferiority when one speaks of visible or invisible religiosity in sociological parlance. However, non-Eurocentric thinkers should be more innovative and attempt to deconstruct democratic discourses which have come to be solely interpreted in reference to dominant Eurocentric ideologies such as social democracy, liberalism or neo-liberalism as there are other ways of conceptualizing democracy which may fall without the parameters of the aforementioned ideologies. In my view, Islamism is such a progressive ideology which could be the alternative model of governance provided it is interpreted within the parameters of democratic principles. These principles are very simple and straightforward, i.e. the source of power within the nation-state society is people and the state should be accountable before the people and transparency should be implemented in all spheres of social life. When we speak of source of power this should not be taken in an absolute fashion. There are many theologically-oriented scholars who aspire to create a bogus conflict by emphasizing the divine source of power. To this argument one could put a counter-argument by stating that we are not talking about the source of power in reality as such. On the contrary, the source of power in a given nation-state which exists as a contingent historical reality which may disappear tomorrow and hence the source of power may shift to another entity. Needless to argue that in many societies today we can talk about the shift of the power-source from the state to multinational corporate companies which do not follow any democratic rule. If these premises are sustainable then one could argue that democratic alternative is the most comprehensive model of political management before us. By critiquing Allama Jafari and scholars who have been oblivious to these fine distinctions between Islamism and Islam, Democracy and Liberalism, and multiple modernities, I have attempted to argue that false comparative strategies may prove useful in short-runs but it will backlash in the long-runs and now the turmoil which have enveloped the entire Muslim World could be understood partially in reference to false comparative strategies. Another important question is the recent discourses of Post-Islamism by scholars such as Asef Bayat who compare the incomparable couple of Islam and Democracy and based on this false dichotomy argue that Islamist movements in Muslim societies are undergoing a post-Islamist turn (Bayat, 1996). It is correct that these movements are undergoing colossal changes but it is too hasty to assume that these transformations are of post-Islamic natures. The problem with these kinds of researches is that scholars who are working within binary frame of references tend to compare incomparable entities. The question is not that within Islamist camps there is no room for change or pluralistic approach. On the contrary, there are many nuances within Islamist discourses but it is wrong to assume that we have entered a new stage which could be considered as a post-Islamist era. The fundamental factors which brought about Islamist discourse to the public square, in the first place, have not changed yet, i.e. people's demand of a visible form of religiosity. Although Bayat himself states that post-Islamism does not necessarily mean the historical end of Islamism but constructing "postness" in conjunction to Islamism along with false dichotomization of Islam and Modernity (Islam and Democracy and so on and so forth) is simply wrong. Because it diverts or even distorts the sociopolitical energies from tackling real issues in the Muslim World, i.e. the process of democratization of Islamism which needs to be taken into consideration as one of the most challenging questions before elites in the Muslim World. In other words, the challenging question is how to democratize Islamism which is, in principle, a progressive ideology as it is Liberalism, Socialism, and other forms of ideologies which create sufficient space for human agency. More importantly, the serious problem with post-Islamist discourses is the fact that if we assume that Islamism has come to its end then what next? Should this mean that we should adopt a secular form of political system? If the answer is affirmative then what should we do about post-secularist discourses which have emerged today in most secularist societies and contexts? To put it differently, the main argument of scholars who argue for post-Islamism is that

> post-Islamism refers to a political and social condition where, following a phase of experimentation, the appeal, energy, and

sources of legitimacy of Islamism get exhausted even among its
once-ardent supporters. (Bayat, 1996)

However the problem with this argument is that the proponents
of this position do not distinguish between various forms of Islamism. Islamism is not a monolithic position in the political landscape
of the Muslim political thought. On the contrary, it is very pluralistic and multifaceted. To argue that Islamism has become exhausted
even among its extreme supporters is a simplistic interpretation of
sociological events on the ground. Bayat mentions Iran as an example (1996) and argues that "Islamism ... both by its own internal
contradictions ... and by societal pressure ... [has become com-
pelled] ... to reinvent itself, but does so ... at the cost of a qualitative shift" (Bayat, 1996). Here Bayat talks about Islamism in a
singular fashion as though there is only one unified version of
Islamism. This is the first critique which comes to mind when
reading Bayat and other scholars who argue for post-Islamism. Secondly, when we talk about the Iranian political system it should be
noted that there is a distinction between Islamism as an ideology
and jurisprudential interpretations of Islamism. We should not
think that this is an irrelevant distinction which could be easily
glossed over. On the contrary, the exhaustion which Bayat refers to
is due to the jurisprudential interpretations of Islamism and those
ardent supporters of Islamism who are allegedly exhausted today—
we need to recast their exhaustion within a more nuanced frame of
theoretical reference. In other words, they are not exhausted from
Islamism as such but they are trying to reconceptualize Islamism
outside the parameters of jurisprudentialist framework. We cannot
understand these theoretical issues if we are oblivious to sociological issues on the ground. This is what I have termed as "visible
religiosity" which seems to determine the political contours of
Muslim societies, politicians and political actors who aspire to
shape, reshape and reform the future political landscape of Iran and
the Muslim World in 21st century. In other words, instead of talking

about post-Islamism and secular strategies in Muslim societies it is more accurate to conceptualize post-Jurisprudential tendencies in conjunction to post-secularist strategies within Islamist frame of references. To put it differently, in order to overcome violent changes and bring about peaceful transformations in the Muslim world we need to design subtle strategies whereby Islamism lends itself more to democratic interpretations rather than elitist or autocratic readings which exclude the pivotal role of "popular sovereignty." Bayat argues that "we may witness for some time the simultaneous process of both Islamization and post-Islamization" (Bayat, 1996).

In the light of what we have argued earlier it is more likely that we shall witness for some time the parallel process of both post-Jurisprudentialization and democratization rather than post-Islamism in the sense Bayat, Gilles Kepel or Olivier Roy have argued. It may be too early to judge as we are very close historically to "Green Movement" which occurred in 2009 but it is undeniable that the aspirations of those who staged and directed this movement were not one of post-Islamization. It is better to view their aspirations as attempts to overcome undemocratic tendencies within Islamism which has relied more heavily on elitist jurisprudentialism rather than leaning on popular authority in running the affairs of the state. Of course it is hard to predict the future but it may not be very farfetched to state that those strategies which are more democratic and within the parameters of Islamism would surely determine the future of Muslim World in 21st century.

Bibliography

Abrahamian, Ervand, Iran Between Two Revolutions, Princeton University Press, 1982.

Alatas, Syed Farid. "Academic Dependency and the Global Division of Labour in the Social Sciences," in *Current Sociology* 51 (6), Nov. 2003; Pp 599–613.

Alatas, Syed Farid. *Alternative Discourses in Asian Social Science: Responses to Eurocentrism*. New Delhi; Thousand Oaks: Sage Publications, 2006.

Bayat, A. "The Coming of a Post-Islamist Society," *Critique: Critical Middle East Studies*, no. 9 (Fall 1996): 43–52.

Brabazon, J. *Albert Schweitzer, Essential Writings*. Orbis Books, New York, 2005.

Casanova, J. *Public Religions in the Modern World*. Chicago: University of Chicago Press, 1994.

Drucker, Peter. *Management: Tasks, Responsibilities, Practices*. New York: Harper & Row, 1974.

Jafari, M. T. *Islamic Mysticism*, Tehran: Center for Allama Jafari Studies, 2013.

Jafari, M. T. *Philosophical Principles of Politics in Islam*, Tehran: Center for Allama Jafari Studies, 2012.

Mintzberg, Henry (ed.). *Mintzberg on Management*. New York, New York: The Free Press Seaver, 1989.

Schweitzer, G. Albert, *The Man and his Mind*, A. & C. Black, London, 1951.

Tibi, B. *Islamism and Islam*. Yale University Press, 2012.

Vaidhyanathan, S. *The Googlization of Everything: (And Why We Should Worry)*, University of California Press, 2011.

CPSIA information can be obtained at www.ICGtesting.com
Printed in the USA
BVOW01*1753110914

366245BV00002B/2/P